This book is one of a collection bequeathed by J. Hugh Campbell, History scholar and instructor at this College from 1975-1982

D1165400

THE GREEK
EXPERIMENT

THE GREEK EXPERIMENT

IMPERIALISM AND SOCIAL CONFLICT
800–400 BC

ROBERT J. LITTMAN

with 93 illustrations, 8 in colour

THAMES AND HUDSON · LONDON

Parentibus Carissimis

Frontispiece: *Nike* (Victory)
crowns a victorious
athlete.

© 1974 THAMES AND HUDSON LTD, LONDON

Printed in Great Britain by Jarrold and Sons Ltd, Norwich

ISBN 0 500 32030 6 *hardcover*
ISBN 0 500 33030 1 *paperback*

CONTENTS

PREFACE

Ever since Plato and Aristotle laid the foundations of Western political theory the Greek city state, the polis, has been romanticized as an ideal social unit for mankind; and the cultural and artistic greatness of city states such as Athens has served in men's eyes to confirm Aristotle's and Plato's admiration for the institution. In this century, however, a more realistic picture of the polis has been developing. While recognizing its cultural greatness we have come to see that as a social institution it was flawed, torn apart by civil war, mistrust and treachery among its citizens. In this book it is my purpose to survey the development of the polis as an institution and to focus on certain of its negative aspects, particularly disunity and civil war within and between city states, and some of their causes, especially restrictive citizenship practices and class struggles.

The organization of this book is by topic, with a rough chronological sequence. Because of this I have at times moved back and forth chronologically, and have repeated some material in different contexts. Owing to the limitations of the series, I have chosen to omit footnotes, and I have taken the liberty at times simply of making decisions on controversial points without arguing them.

Directly and indirectly this work owes much to the labours of other scholars, many of whom are listed in the bibliography. I am indebted to many friends and colleagues who have read this book in manuscript and provided useful criticism. I am particularly grateful to Professors F. Zeitlin, M. Smith, G. Highet, H. Nader, N. Cantor and A. Cameron, and to Dr A. Cameron; and especially to Professor L. A. Losada for allowing me to see his recently published *The Fifth Column in the Peloponnesian War* (Leiden, 1972) while it was still in manuscript. Professor Geoffrey Barraclough, the General Editor of this series, has also rendered invaluable guidance and criticism. The person without whose support this book truly would have been impossible is my wife Bernice.

University of Hawaii
Honolulu

Robert J. Littman

7

I DISUNITY AND THE GREEK CHARACTER

Historians of ancient Greece have tended to dwell on its achievements, on the legacy of ideas it handed down to Europe, on its culture and civilization and on the contribution of Athens to political thought. The present work follows a different course. It is not that the achievements were not great. But a one-sided emphasis on the Greek cultural legacy is apt to obscure other aspects of Greek experience, and there is as much to be learned from a critical analysis of Greek society – from studying the problems with which it had to cope and seeing how far it came up with valid answers, and, where it did not, why not – as there is from the more conventional attempt to allot it a place in the development of 'Western tradition'. Modern historians are less interested in 'linear history', in tracing the transmission of ideas from generation to generation, than in analytical history, which investigates the social forces at play within a given society and the interaction of social groups. In this way, they believe, it is possible to cast light on the operation of social processes, which, however different the particular circumstances may be, are a common part of human experience.

Anyone approaching classical Greece in this way is at once confronted by a great paradox. It may be, as E. R. Bevan once wrote, that 'what we call the Western Spirit is really Hellenism re-incarnate'. But politically the Greek city state – the political unit in which that spirit was born – was ultimately a failure. Its history is one of dissent and disunity, of war between Greek cities and within the cities themselves. During the ninth and eighth centuries BC the polis flourished as a kinship-based agricultural society, divided into aristocrats and peasants. So long as trade and commerce were minimal the fragmentation and factionalism which existed did not prevent the polis from being an effective unit. But in the late eighth and early seventh centuries rapid increases in the size of population and the rise of trade forced the polis out of its isolation; it could no longer function efficiently as an individual agricultural state, cut off from its neighbours. However, the polis had little flexibility. As a unicellular organism, incapable of

9

3 Odysseus and the swineherd Eumaios. Early Greek society was almost exclusively agricultural, with a strict near-feudal division between the aristocrats and the peasantry.

growth except by subdivision, it could reproduce indefinitely; but its offspring could not combine with it to form a united creature. Consequently it could not successfully adapt to a changing world.

Economic and social developments in Greece during the seventh and sixth centuries plunged the polis into political and social chaos. The fifth century saw the beginnings of new forms of government, which transcended the polis and were capable of uniting several states: the Athenian empire and the Peloponnesian League, to be followed in the fourth century by Panhellenism and further attempts at union through powerful leagues. These experiments failed: disunity was so ingrained that even the descending armies of Philip of Macedon could not induce the Greek city states to stand together. Unification had to come from without, imposed by Philip and after him Alexander. Even then, a truly stable unity did not come to Greece until the country was garrisoned by Rome in 146 BC.

4 View from Delphi towards the Gulf of Itea. Mountainous terrain is the usual pattern in Greece, and this particular view, with its thick growth of olive trees, must have looked much the same 2,500 years ago as it does today.

The disunity of Greece has been explained by many theories, but none is altogether satisfactory. Many have suggested that the geography of the land was a major factor in preventing unity. Greek settlements extended through Asia Minor, the islands of the Aegean and mainland Greece. The coast of the entire area is jagged and the land broken by bays and gulfs; the interior is full of mountains and mountainous districts, producing many small separated regions. This physical fragmentation is believed to have prompted the development of highly individual city states.

Though such a view is attractive, it is simplistic. Geography doubtless played some part in Greece's political development, but the extent of its influence is easy to overrate. The patterns of Greek settlement throw some light on the question. Regardless of the nature of the land, wherever Greeks settled they were disunited. The colonies they founded in southern Italy, such as Croton and Tarentum, became

5, 6 Sport offered an important outlet for the competitive obsession of the Greek character and provided an inspiration for much art and literature. Here bareback riding and boxing are depicted on Attic vases, one of them

independent states. Yet when Rome expanded south in the third century BC she had little difficulty in welding southern Italy into a cohesive area. Step by step, Rome assimilated and incorporated first Italy and then the entire Mediterranean into the Roman state. Inherently the Romans unified and the Greeks produced only disunity. A further flaw in the geographical theory is the fact that it was in just those regions where the physical barriers were minimal that the polis flourished best, while in the more mountainous regions, such as Arcadia, it was slow in developing. Many other lands and countries fragmented by nature never formed a polis system.

Furthermore, though geography may have encouraged fragmentation in Greece and the nature of the land may be consistent with the formation of many independent states, still unexplained is the constant strife and dissension that was ingrained in every Greek city,

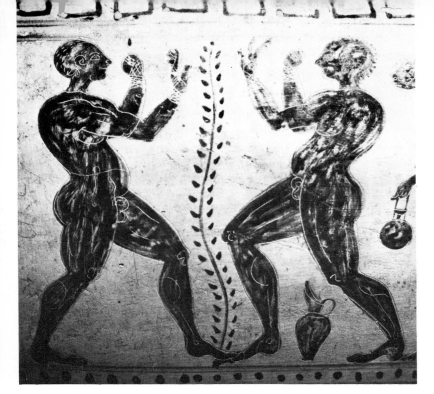

(left) an amphora presented to a victor at the Panathenaia, a local Athenian festival transformed by the tyrant Peisistratus into a great Panhellenic contest which brought both prestige and wealth to his city.

where class struggles, civil war, treason, betrayal and constant contention were the norm. Many factors contributed to disunity. It is beyond the scope of this study to analyse the Greek character, but one facet of it stands out as at least partly responsible for disunity, both on a national level and on that of the individual city. The Greeks were one of the most competitive peoples in history. Everything was made into a contest, from athletics to the great drama festivals, such as the Dionysia at Athens, where playwrights vied for prizes. Competition was formalized in the great *agones*, public festivals at which competitors contended. The prizes for victory were generally of symbolic value only, though the victor might incidentally receive rich rewards from his city. According to the historian Herodotus, certain Arcadians who had deserted the Greek cause for the Persian and been brought before Xerxes, King of Persia, were asked what the Greeks were doing

13

at that moment; they replied that they were celebrating the Olympic festival and viewing sports and horse-races. Xerxes then inquired as to the prize. When the Arcadians responded that it was a crown of olive, a Persian broke into the inquisition: 'My god, Mardonius, what sort of men are these against whom you have brought us to fight? They do not compete for money, but for glory.' Usually these competitions were religious in origin, under the patronage of some god. The best known were the Panhellenic athletic contests, the Olympian, Pythian, Nemean and Isthmian Games. The Greeks even competed in singing, in riddle-solving, in staying awake, in dancing.

Much of the competition, however, was non-productive. The Greeks had a shame culture, rather than a guilt culture. In the former one's sense of worth is entirely determined by the opinion of others, while in the latter an internalized set of standards control behaviour. As in many shame cultures, the Greeks regarded any kind of defeat as disgraceful, regardless of circumstances. Yet no victory was possible unless someone else lost. The glory of winning accrued to the victor from the lost glory of the defeated. The loser could not leave the contest with as much prestige as he entered. Contributing to this contentiousness was the Greek obsession with fame, honour and achievement.

The competitiveness of the Greeks was rooted in their narcissism, which led them into a continuing struggle for personal glory and fame, as well as for the wealth and power by means of which these were to be acquired. Personal ambition was unquenchable. Such men as the Athenian Alcibiades were paradigmatic of the Greek ideal and of the tragic self-destructiveness which was inherent in that ideal. During the Peloponnesian War, for example, to create opportunities for his own self-aggrandizement, Alcibiades encouraged Athens to send him to open a second front with the Sicilian Expedition at a time when renewed war with Sparta might erupt at any moment. Then one night, shortly before the Expedition was to depart for Sicily, the faces and phalli of the small stone statues called 'herms', which stood in front of many houses, were found to have been mutilated. At the same time it came to light that Alcibiades and others had not only been parodying the secret ceremonies of the Eleusinian Mysteries, sacred rites celebrated in honour of Demeter and Persephone, but had even allowed persons uninitiated into those rites to learn their secrets by witnessing the parody. His involvement in the ensuing accusations of sacrilege caused Alcibiades to be relieved of his command of the Sicilian venture, whereupon, his sense of personal worth violated, he

7 The Persian King Darius trampling on his enemies. The powerful Persian presence on the eastern edge of their world acted both as a stimulus to unity among the Greeks and as a focus and haven for dissident elements.

deserted to Sparta to fight against Athens. After seeking glory in this arena for a time, however, he left Sparta for Persia, and finally returned to Athens. But he quit Athens once again, this time to fight as a privateer in the Thracian region, in which capacity he made one last attempt to regain the honour he desperately sought by coming to the aid of his native city. His proffered help was rejected, however, and within a short time, while on his way to Persia, he was killed (at the instigation of the Spartans, who wanted him out of the way as an ever possible saviour of Athens).

Alcibiades was a loyal Athenian, but loyal to Athens only when Alcibiades was running its affairs. The same motivation is seen in the actions of the oligarchs at Athens, who in 404 BC preferred to betray their city to Sparta rather than see democrats rule it. Betrayal and treason were national pastimes of the Greeks. When deposed, Hippias, tyrant of Athens, went over to the Persians and fought with them at the battle of Marathon against Athens and Greece. When Demaratus, King of Sparta, was expelled by his co-monarch, he fled to Persia and aided invading Persian armies against his homeland. Themistocles, who had been the architect of the Persian defeat in the Persian War, eventually deserted Athens for Persia, where he enjoyed a successful career. 'I fear the Greeks, even bearing gifts' had much basis in reality.

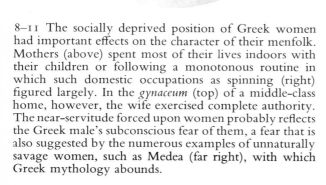

8–11 The socially deprived position of Greek women had important effects on the character of their menfolk. Mothers (above) spent most of their lives indoors with their children or following a monotonous routine in which such domestic occupations as spinning (right) figured largely. In the *gynaceum* (top) of a middle-class home, however, the wife exercised complete authority. The near-servitude forced upon women probably reflects the Greek male's subconscious fear of them, a fear that is also suggested by the numerous examples of unnaturally savage women, such as Medea (far right), with which Greek mythology abounds.

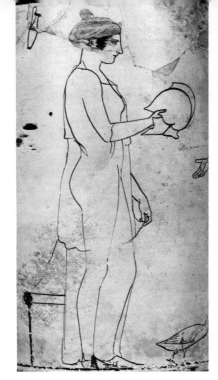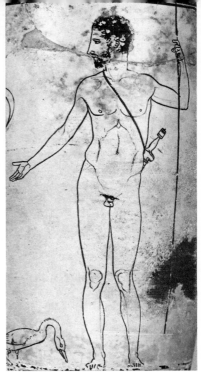

The Greeks were obsessively concerned with the admiration and approval of their peers. This fostered a character which was vain, boastful, ambitious, envious and vindictive. Above all the arousal of envy and the obtaining of revenge were esteemed most highly. Thucydides, the historian of the Peloponnesian War, observes in connection with civil strife:

> Words had to change their ordinary meaning and to take that which was now given them. Reckless audacity came to be considered the courage of a loyal ally; prudent hesitation, specious cowardice; moderation was held to be a cloak for unmanliness; the ability to see all sides of a question, a sign of incapacity to act on any. Frantic violence became the attribute of manliness. . . . Revenge also was held of more account than self-preservation. Oaths of reconciliation . . . only held good so long as no other weapon was at hand; but, when opportunity offered, he who first ventured to seize it and to take his enemy off his guard thought this perfidious vengeance sweeter than an open one, since, considerations of safety apart, success by treachery won him the palm of superior intelligence.

12–14 Left, a submissive wife handing her husband his helmet as he prepares for battle. Above, fighting warrior whose mother stands behind him, perhaps unconsciously reflecting the Greek mother's ambiguous role.

Indeed it is generally the case that honest men are readier to call rogues clever than simpletons honest. . . . The cause of all these evils was the lust for rule arising from greed and ambition.

It has recently been suggested by Philip Slater in *The Glory of Hera* (Boston, 1968) that narcissism in Greek society may have been a product of the family structure. Women, together with slaves, were considered inferior by nature, as Aristotle so bluntly put it. Consequently they were relegated to child-bearing and domestic duties. They had few legal rights, received little or no education, were excluded from male society, and were largely confined to the home. A wife who ate in the company of men was viewed as a prostitute. In general the socially accepted attitude towards women was one of contempt. A woman could not be older than her husband, nor receive the same pay for the same job as a male. In the house, however, she was supreme: she controlled the women's quarters, the inhabitants of which included the children and slaves.

At a young age the Greek girl passed from her father's house to that of her husband, who had been chosen by her father. Since the Greek male married late and the woman early, a typical bride might be sixteen and her husband thirty. Often a brother-sister instead of a connubial relationship existed between husband and wife. The wife was usually ignored by her husband, whose real love might be public life, business, his male social companions or the *hetairai*, educated courtesans similar in many ways to the Japanese geisha. So Pericles, entranced by the *hetaira* Aspasia, left his wife for her. Slater asserts that the wife could and did take out on her male child the resentment she felt towards her husband. There was great antagonism between the sexes and the mother thus became ambivalent towards her son. She tried to make him a replacement for her husband, but at the same time she made him a scapegoat. She thus at the same time exalted and belittled her son, and fed on and destroyed him. On the one hand she accepted him as a hero and on the other she rejected him. This produced a person overly concerned with his image in the minds of others and with an unstable self-concept: a person who was fearful of women. This fear is reflected in the terrifying and vengeful portraits of women in Greek tragedy and myth, women such as Medea, who murders her children, and Clytemnestra, who kills her husband. Most of the monsters of mythology are earth-born females – the Medusa, Scylla and Charybdis, the Furies. When Zeus decided to punish man because Prometheus had stolen fire, the worst penalty he could devise was 'the damnable race of women . . . a plague with which men must live'. Uranus was castrated by Cronos while he was having intercourse with Gaia, who provided her son with the weapon and set the ambush. The Greek man felt that he was a hero or nothing. Pride, prestige and honour were paramount. In short the Greek male became the classic narcissist. Vanity and a concern with physical appearance and the externals of life were overly important, and homosexuality and bisexuality, commonly associated with narcissism, were widespread, at least among members of the upper classes, such as Alcibiades and Plato.

Egoism, the Greek need to excel, to gain honour and glory at the expense of others, helped to produce a society incapable of unity. The individual would not risk sacrificing himself for the city state, nor the city state for the welfare of all Greece. This facet of Greek character must be regarded as a major contribution to Greek contentiousness.

While the competitive nature of the Greeks may have generated innumerable political problems, it also stimulated creative genius in art, literature, philosophy and science in certain respects never since

15 A bearded adult kisses his younger boy-friend. The prevalence of narcissism and homosexuality, idealized by many Greek writers as a more refined passion than the love of a man for a woman, was closely linked with the suspicious contempt in which Greek women were held.

equalled. The concentration of achievement in fifth- and fourth-century Greece was astounding. Socrates, Plato, Hippocrates, Polycleitus, Praxiteles, Thucydides, Herodotus, Aeschylus, Sophocles and Euripides were all products of Greek society, along with its contentiousness, factionalism, civil wars and disunity.

Many factors encouraged disunity in Greece, among them the social framework and the economic and political patterns of development. The character of the Greeks may have been consonant with disunity, but the cause and effect is impossible to determine. The Romans were superb at organization and unification, yet many centuries after the fall of Rome Italy polarized into numerous powerful city states. Did the 'character' of the Italians change or did different political and socio-economic factors cause the city-state system to develop in Italy? Greek contentiousness and competitiveness contributed to disunity, but at the same time the political, economic and social structure encouraged and fostered those very traits. Thus, while the competitive nature of the Greek character can be considered neither as the cause of Greek disunity, nor necessarily as a direct result of it, their political system formed a fertile culture medium in which contentiousness could breed.

II THE GREEK CITY STATE

Aristotle wrote that 'man is by nature a political animal'. His meaning was not that man likes to battle in the arena of politics, but that man is a creature whose nature it is to live in a 'polis'. The 'polis' represented more than a political concept; the usual translation, 'city state', fails to convey this. Babylon might have been labelled a city state in its early period, but it was in no sense a 'polis'. 'Polis' means the total society and civilization of the Greek state.

The word itself originally meant the citadel where the centre of the state was located, but it came to be applied to the entire state, to the people and to the culture of the state. A polis often took its name from its citizens: in Greek the word for the polis of Athens was 'the Athenians'. Thucydides wrote 'the citizens are the polis'. In his funeral oration over those who had died in the first year of the Peloponnesian War Pericles presented an idealized view of Athens: 'We throw our polis open to all the world.' Polis means here not just the political organization, but the city in all its aspects, its culture, its military structure, its society and its way of life. Having spoken of the character of the Athenian people, their attitudes towards political involvement, their constitution, their military training, their nobility of spirit, their love of beauty and wisdom, Pericles summed it all up: 'in a word, then, I say that our polis as a whole is the school of Hellas.'

In the second century AD the traveller Pausanias complained that a certain city of the Phocians barely deserved to be called a polis because it lacked government buildings, a gymnasium, a theatre, a market-place and piped water. Though Pausanias was writing seven hundred years after the great age of the polis, he reflected the Greek attitude towards the polis as a centre of civilization.

Aristotle saw the polis as the natural unit for human existence 'and a man that is by nature and not by fortune citiless [*apolis*] is either subhuman or superhuman'. The institution of the polis separated Greeks from barbarians and on this basis Aristotle could place the latter in the same category as slaves. For Aristotle and the Greeks the

23

polis represented civilization, inseparable parts of which were justice and law. Aristotle said, 'as man is the best of animals when perfected, so he is the worst of all when sundered from law and justice.'

The *Oresteia* of Aeschylus well illustrates the idea of justice and the polis. This trilogy of plays reflects the conflict between the old blood law of vengeance and retribution and the enlightened justice of the polis. In the *Agamemnon*, the first play of the trilogy, Agamemnon returns from the Trojan War to his kingdom at Argos and his wife Clytemnestra, with Cassandra, of the royal house of Priam, as his captive concubine. Jealous of Cassandra and eager to avenge the death of their daughter, Iphigenia (who had been mercilessly sacrificed by her father at Aulis ten years earlier in an effort to procure favourable winds for the Greek fleet), Clytemnestra hacks her husband to death in his bath with an axe, and dispatches Cassandra. By the old laws, the first crime calls for another crime to avenge it. Until there is retribution for the murder of a relative, pollution and blood guilt hang over the family of the slain.

In the *Libation-Bearers*, the second play of the trilogy, Orestes is commanded by Apollo to take vengeance on his father's murderers

17 Relief probably depicting the murder of Aegisthus by Orestes. Aeschylus transformed an archaic story into an allegory presenting the Athenian polis as an ideal social system in which natural forces (the Furies) and enlightened rationalism (the Olympians) were reconciled.

18 The concept of *Dike* (Justice) was central to Greek political thought. Here an allegorical struggle between *Dike* and *Adikia* (Injustice) is depicted on an early red-figure vase.

lest the Furies rise from the earth to haunt and harass him, to scourge his bruised and bleeding, execrated body from the land and force him to wander, an outcast hateful to men and unloved, to die at last, shrunken and wasted in a painful death. Zeus gives approval to the deed, for justice cries out for the punishment of murder. As the god of civilization, of the polis, of justice, of enlightenment, Apollo gives the order to Orestes.

The *Libation-Bearers* ends with Orestes avenging his father's murder by the slaughter of his mother. Clytemnestra has to die, since by murdering her husband, the king, she has destroyed family ties and struck at social order. However, those same Furies which would have pursued Orestes if he had left his father unavenged, now cry out for his blood since he has profaned the blood-tie by the murder of his mother. In the *Eumenides*, the last play of the trilogy, the Furies, the guardians of the old tribal justice, battle with the Olympian gods, the gods of the polis and civilization. Orestes flees the avenging Furies and takes refuge on the acropolis at Athens. Athena now comes with a compromise from Zeus: Orestes will be tried by a jury of Athenian citizens. Arguments are presented on both sides, for justice and mercy on the one hand, and blood vengeance on the other, and

25

the jury deadlocks in its vote, symbolizing the equal claims of natural law and primitive vengeance on the one hand, and the order and justice of civilized society on the other. As the foreman of the jury Athena holds the deciding vote, and casts it for Orestes. At this the Furies threaten to destroy Athens, but Athena persuades them to complement rather than oppose the polis. The polis cannot exist without the primal forces of natural justice, nor can it exist with the chaos which they produce. Thus the Furies must be transmuted into the 'Kindly Ones', the Eumenides, to punish violence and outrages against nature in the polis, as well as in the family, and become the defenders of the new social order of justice and the polis.

The polis developed gradually out of the ashes of Mycenaean civilization. About 2000 BC the first Greeks poured into Greece, vanquishing the native population as they came. These Greeks, whom we call the Mycenaeans after their chief citadel, spread their culture to the remotest corners of Greece. They built monumental cities on a scale so large and involving such feats of engineering that later Greeks believed Mycenaean masonry to have been constructed by the mythical race of giants, the Cyclopes. During the Mycenaean period Greece reached an economic peak.

19–21 Left, the so-called Treasury of Atreus at Mycenae. Mycenaean culture displays a barbaric splendour (the inner lintel of this door has been estimated to weigh 100 tons) very different from the delicacy of the typical Cretan style, represented here by the throne room of the Palace at Cnossos and a

At the time of the Mycenaean entry into Greece there was already a large and highly civilized culture in the Aegean, centred on Crete. This culture is called Minoan, after the legendary King Minos. During the Early Minoan period (c. 3000–2100 BC) the Minoans extended their flourishing overseas trade as far as Egypt. The quantity of gold and jewellery found in Minoan sites of this period shows the prosperity and extent of this trade. About 2000 BC great cities centred around unfortified palaces grew up in Crete, the greatest of which was the so-called 'Palace of Minos' at Cnossos. Under the stimulus of foreign influence brought by trade, Minoan civilization rapidly advanced. Minoan ships sailed along the entire eastern Mediterranean coast, Egypt and southern Anatolia and the Aegean islands.

Political unrest and warfare in the Near East in the eighteenth and seventeenth centuries BC, however, produced a drastic reduction in Minoan trade. Forced to broaden their markets, the Minoans turned more and more to Greece, a shift which is evidenced by the Minoan influence on Greek pottery. About 1600 BC Cnossos was struck by a devastating earthquake, as it had been in about 1750 BC; but each time it quickly recovered. Under the stimulation and influence of Minoan culture, the Mycenaeans built up their own highly developed

cup decorated with a wasp-waisted, long-haired prince from Hagia Triada. Nevertheless Cretan influence is clearly visible in the remains of the Mycenaean citadels and after the fall of Cnossos the rapidly developing cities of mainland Greece did much to preserve Minoan traditions.

trading empire, which in the sixteenth and fifteenth centuries was successfully competing with the Minoans in Egypt. With the destruction of the palace at Cnossos about 1400 BC – perhaps by another earthquake, perhaps by a Mycenaean invasion, or by the effects of a volcanic eruption on the island of Thera – the Mycenaeans seized the dominant trading and commercial position in the Mediterranean.

The height of Mycenaean power extended from the end of the fifteenth to the end of the thirteenth century. About 1230 BC its collapse began with the destruction of Pylos by unknown hands. Almost simultaneously other centres of Mycenaean civilization fell. At Mycenae and Athens the people withdrew into the citadel and held out against the wave of destruction. Mycenaean power, wealth and culture, however, though severely truncated, survived. Greece was not the only area affected by the disruptions of this period. In the Near East, the Hittite empire was destroyed at the beginning of the twelfth century BC. Mycenaean trade in the East all but ceased. Mycenae itself survived only for another hundred years, when the city was sacked and burned. Apart from some isolated survivals of Mycenaean culture, Greece at this time began her Dark Ages.

The cause of the upheavals is uncertain. In the last century the prevalent theory was that a group of Greeks called Dorians, after the dialect which they spoke, invaded and destroyed the Mycenaean empire. However, archaeological evidence now suggests to many that though the Dorian Greeks may have begun their migrations into Greece about this time, their entrance was largely peaceful and extended over several centuries, with the concentration of their settlements in southern Greece and the islands, especially the Peloponnesus, Crete and Rhodes. Another hypothesis is that the mysterious Sea Peoples, probably Greeks who had fought as mercenaries for Egypt and against the Hittites and later, at the beginning of the twelfth century, against a Hittite-Egyptian alliance, were responsible for the destruction of Mycenaean citadels in a series of piratical raids. The true answer remains unknown, but certain facts are incontrovertible: Mycenaean centres were violently destroyed at the end of the thirteenth century BC; the Hittite empire fell in the twelfth century but its conquerors were repelled from Egypt; new peoples settled in the Mediterranean; and Mycenaean trade was destroyed in the East, though some traces were still found in the West.

Mycenaean power had been concentrated in individual kingdoms, whose centres were fortified cities, such as Mycenae and Pylos. The core of each city was a strong walled citadel where the royal palace stood. Round the citadel and under its protection an unfortified town usually flourished. From this centre the king might control many neighbouring towns, whose vassal rulers were subject to him.

With the fall of the Mycenaean states, the kingship gradually died out and its power was usurped by an aristocracy – although some vestiges of monarchy remained in many states, such as Sparta, where the hereditary kingship, with powers somewhat curtailed, continued until the third century BC. Tribal divisions reasserted themselves and by the end of the ninth century two political units, the tribal state and the polis, had come to the fore. The tribal state was formed from a number of loosely knit villages and towns originally settled by a single tribe. Its origin was in the periods of migration during which a tribe settled a particular area, as the Achaeans did in Achaea. Very often the country assumed its name from the tribe, such as Locris and Achaea. The tribal state lacked cohesive political organization and remained both economically and culturally primitive. Although districts might occasionally opt for independence, the unity of the tribe persisted and was reinforced by a common centre of worship of the tribal god.

The polis became a small close-knit urban political unit. A natural fortification, usually a dominating hill called an 'acropolis' (literally 'high city'), was chosen as its centre. Often this was on the site of a Mycenaean citadel, but the polis at this stage of its existence was a mere shadow of its predecessor. In Crete, for example, nearly a hundred city states replaced the previous unity of the island. This meant a hundred constitutions, a hundred armies, a hundred governments. At the foot of the citadel was the agora or market-place, as well as the homes of most of the people, who normally walked to work in their fields and lived in the town. The citadel became the religious centre of the state, with temples to the state god. A wall, encompassing the citadel, the agora, and some open space, usually surrounded the main town. Within the wall were also the temples, the state cults and the government buildings.

The polis was, however, much more than merely the main walled town; it also included the town's hinterland. Athens provides a good example. The polis of Athens was not just the city, but the whole of Attica, an area of about a thousand square miles (about the size of Luxemburg). Athenian legend said that Theseus had united Attica under one rule, but the unification was actually a gradual process by

22 The arrival of Theseus in Athens. City states commonly adopted demi-gods and mythological figures as national heroes, in order to focus patriotic sentiment and demonstrate the divine favour they enjoyed.

which Athens reduced small cities and made them part of the state, and it was not completed until perhaps the eighth century when neighbouring Eleusis was incorporated into the polis. All native residents of Attica were citizens of the polis. The religious and political centres of the state were in the town, where the assemblies met, and where the people gathered to exercise their franchise. Many maritime states were not actually situated on the water, but a few miles inland, as was the case with Athens. Her port, the Piraeus, was about three miles distant from the acropolis. Eventually, in the mid-fifth century, the city walls were extended to encompass the port, which by this time had grown into a busy and thriving trading centre.

In writing of his ideal polis, modelled on the actual institution, Aristotle insisted on 'unity of place'. The land should be large enough for the state to be self-sufficient and for the inhabitants to live a life of liberal and temperate leisure. It should be well situated in relation to sea and country, be in communication with all parts of the territory for the purpose of sending out military assistance and be easily accessible for the conveyance to it of agricultural produce. The land should be difficult for enemies to invade and easy to defend. The pattern of Greek city states reflects Aristotle's ideal. Besides those cities centred round an acropolis, peninsulas, offshore islands and other easily defensible areas were favoured sites.

Sparta held the largest territory of any polis, nearly 3,300 square miles, which was more than twice the size of the next largest and over three times that of any other polis in mainland Greece. Her unusual size may be explained by her particular governmental and social structure, which set her apart from other city states and made her virtually a territorial state. As was the case in other city states, the city itself was the political centre. The state was controlled by a small hard core of Spartan citizens called Spartiates, who spent their lives as professional soldiers and kept in subjugation the population of their territory, which consisted mostly of serfs, known as 'helots', who cultivated the land.

Apart from Athens and Sparta, few city states in mainland Greece exceeded 400 square miles in area, which is about half the size of New York City. Delos was among the smallest with 2 square miles, the size of Gibraltar. Corinth held 340 square miles, Aegina 33, Samos 180. The district of Phocis, covering 630 square miles, comprised twenty-two city states. The city states of south Italy and Sicily, where the land was not quite so fragmented by nature, controlled greater territories, the largest of which were Syracuse with 1,830 square miles and Acragas with 1,670.

The population of the polis was also small. Ideally, according to Aristotle, each citizen should be able to recognize his fellow citizens by sight. In his view the smallest population for a state was that which both allowed it to be self-sufficient and enabled its members to live well. Too large a state, although self-sufficient, was thought to be unmanageable. Thus a polis of 10 citizens would be as impossible as one of 100,000. For Plato the ideal state had 5,000 citizens. This would produce a population of about 50,000, allowing for wives, children, slaves and non-citizens. In practice many city states had fewer than 5,000 citizens, and only three had citizen populations exceeding 20,000 – Syracuse and Acragas in Sicily and Athens in mainland Greece. At the height of her growth, just before the outbreak of the Peloponnesian War, Athens had about 40,000 citizens and a total

23 Mainland Greece in the fifth century BC

population of some 300,000, including women, children, slaves and other non-citizens. The variation in population of city states was great, with a mean of about 10,000 citizens for the most powerful states (a figure the town-planner Hippodamus labelled as ideal).

Aristotle defined the polis as 'a partnership of families and of clans in living well . . . its object is a full and independent life'. At its roots the polis remained a sophisticated tribal and kinship organization. Internal divisions into three or four tribes existed in almost all Greek states. The tribes provided the basic administrative and military unit of the state. As the polis developed, ties between a tribe in one city and the same tribe in another became very weak, and tribal kinship became important only within a city state. Although tribes began as kinship relations of common descent, the city states, gradually and at different times, changed the basis of tribe membership to one of locality. Even after such a reformation, however, tribal membership often remained hereditary, as at Athens.

The two smaller kinship divisions which were constituents of the tribe were the 'phratries' (brotherhoods) and clans. All citizens of classical Athens were members of a phratry, which was responsible for marriages, adoption, births and religious worship. After the late fourth century, as Athenian society began to lose its kinship characteristics, the phratries gradually died out. In Athens, and probably in many other city states, the clans were composed exclusively of aristocrats, although they may once have included all the free inhabitants of Attica. Every clan had its own cult and in some cases particular clans exclusively provided the priests for state cults. In the earlier period of the polis the clan served as the basis for aristocratic power, but as the tribal division came to be the primary force in the political organization of the polis they lost their political importance, though retaining great social prestige. Consequently, they survived the demise of the kinship system and endured into Roman times. The smallest unit in the state was the family, composed of the nuclear family of husband, wife and children, the extended family, and dependants, including slaves.

Although the Greeks possessed a common language, a common heritage, and a common religious pantheon with Zeus at its head, city states developed great religious differences, including their own cults, which served to reinforce the separation of city states. Athena Polias 'the Protector', for example, was the patron goddess of Athens, but at Sparta she was worshipped as a lesser goddess, Athena of the

Brazen House. Argos made Hera the city's god, while at Athens she retained her function as the goddess of the home. Further, there existed vast numbers of local shrines in the countryside, dedicated to major gods or to local heroes, which served as religious centres for families and phratries, and provided further religious disunity.

The kinship and tribal structures, religious differences and, most important, the isolation of early city states from one another led to the creation of restrictive citizenship practices. Although hospitality rights protected strangers – and Zeus in one of his attributes was their guardian – anyone from outside the community was looked on with apprehension, even if he came from a polis a few miles away. Strangers were enemies. Sparta, the most extreme example, forbade foreigners to reside within her territory. When this attitude became somewhat relaxed a few foreigners settled there, but they were periodically expelled. Even in fifth-century Athens foreigners and their descendants were outsiders who were scarcely ever admitted to citizenship, although they comprised over 10 per cent of the population and incurred most of the obligations of citizens.

Hostility towards and fear of outsiders are almost universal traits, reflected in the language many cultures use to refer to those who are not members of their group. The ancient Egyptians, according to Herodotus, called those who did not speak their language 'barbarians'. The Chinese at one time called all foreigners 'devils'. The Hebrews referred to the rest of the world as 'goyim', a word which originally meant 'nations' but soon came to be restricted to non-Jews and took on derogatory connotations. The Greeks labelled someone who did not speak Greek as a *barbaros*, which at first meant someone who spoke unintelligibly, that is who spoke any language but Greek. But by the fifth century BC the word had taken on all the connotations of our 'barbarian'. Hellenized Jews even referred to non-Jews as *barbaroi*, an ironic usage since a few centuries earlier they themselves would have borne this name. The enlightened Aristotle quoted with approval Euripides' statement that 'it is right and reasonable that Greeks should rule over barbarians', and added 'for the latter are by nature slaves and the former free men'.

Besides the natural feelings of exclusiveness which the early Greek polis shared with many other local or ethnic groupings, but which was reinforced by lack of contact with other states, the entire social and religious fabric of kinship relations, clans and clan cults among the Greeks prevented the outsider from assuming a position of equality in society and kept him a stranger within the gates. The position of the stranger was further aggravated by his inability to acquire land, which was entirely in the hands of the tribes and which only members of a tribe could own. In the earlier periods land (or at least a certain portion of it) was often difficult to alienate. This situation continued possibly until as late as the fifth century in some states such as Sparta, where the original stretch of land assigned by the state at birth was inalienable. Thus it was almost impossible for foreigners to acquire land, and even when and where land could be sold, they were usually forbidden to buy it. While in some states ownership of land might be the basic requirement for citizenship, usually the size of one's land-holdings determined voting rights and the offices that one could hold. Later in some states this qualification was to be replaced by the amount of one's personal wealth.

A basic requirement for citizenship was membership in a tribe and clan. The administration of the government, especially the election of magistrates, was connected with the tribe. By and large the only means of admission into a tribe was to be born of members of that tribe. In some places the rule of descent was very strict, requiring that one be born of two citizen parents or one citizen parent and a foreigner from a city with which one's city had a special treaty of marriage. In Athens the rule that marriage between a citizen and a foreigner produced a non-citizen was introduced in the fifth century. In many states, however, especially those such as Cyrene which bordered on foreign lands, such marriages were legal and frequent. In more liberal cities (such as Athens in the seventh and sixth centuries) numbers of foreigners at times gained citizenship through their association with the tyrant of the city, especially as tribe and kinship relations were reduced to legal fictions with the expansion of the city state.

The polis could confer citizenship for some special contribution to the common good. Until the fourth century this was generally done only for those who had lost citizenship in their own states. States at times withdrew citizenship, which might force a person into exile, but this extreme penalty was invoked only for major political or religious offences. A state could at times revise its citizenship lists, as Athens did in the purge of 451/450 BC, thereby depriving certain people of their citizenship.

Citizenship carried with it economic advantages, particularly, as we have seen, that of owning land. But it meant more than this, it meant membership in a political and social community. Since participation in political life was so widespread in such cities as Athens, to be excluded from it cut the stranger off from an important part of the city's life. A non-citizen might be entertained in anyone's home and might befriend citizens, but he was barred from many of the organizations, such as the clan, which though religious and political in nature also played an important social role. In modern Europe or America, where citizenship confers merely the privilege of voting periodically and serving in office (which only a minuscule number of people are able to do), a non-citizen can easily lead the life of a citizen. But in classical Greece a non-citizen was excluded not only from political life, but also from many religious and social aspects of the state. In short, the foreigner in a city state was an outsider without a niche in a society where everyone had his price.

About 10 per cent of the population in a city state were full citizens. (Only adult males could be counted as full citizens.) The percentage varied considerably according to whether the state was an oligarchy or democracy and to how liberal the régime was. Two tendencies were at work in most states, the desire on the part of the people for equality and the conflicting desire to limit citizenship to a few, which tended to favour the rich and powerful oligarchs. Oligarchy was the usual form of government in sixth-century Greece, except in Athens and in the places under her sway. In the fifth century, the great conflict between oligarchy and democracy reached a climax. And yet in Greece oligarchy and democracy were essentially the same form of government. All the citizens with full rights ruled under both systems, but an oligarchy had a smaller percentage than did a democracy. An oligarchy was thus a democracy of a small number of citizens.

Although a woman was technically a citizen, she had virtually no political rights. In most cities she could not usually appear in court without a male spokesman, nor could she own or inherit property; and in no city could she vote. In Athens almost her only right was that her offspring could be citizens, provided she was married to a citizen. In Sparta and in some other states, however, women could own property, and in Gortyn, a leading city of Crete, they could even appear in court on their own behalf. Citizenship was further limited by age, eighteen to twenty-one being the age of majority. Often a man could not hold office or take up full membership in the governing body politic until he reached the age of thirty. One had to be at least sixty to serve in the Spartan senate.

24 The hoplite method of warfare, besides giving non-aristocrats a new fighting potential and so greater political weight, also imposed a novel concept of discipline and uniformity in warfare. Whereas the Homeric hero had prided himself on sporting distinctive armour, these late sixth-century soldiers carry identical shields, each decorated with a sacred tripod.

Certain classes of adult male citizens had only limited political rights. The members of the lower classes might be nominally citizens, but they were at first excluded from all political power. To a great extent this was due to the prevailing method of warfare. Those who did not take part in the defence of the state had insufficient bargaining power to press successfully for a vote in its government. As methods of warfare changed, beginning in about 700 BC with the introduction of the 'hoplite' or heavy-armed infantryman, a greater proportion of citizens gradually came to participate in warfare and accordingly gained voting and office-holding rights. In early sixth-century Athens, for example, the *thetes*, the lowest class of citizens, could not hold office, although they could vote in the popular assembly. When Athens later became dependent on sea power in the fifth century, the *thetes* finally gained full rights, for they manned the fleet.

Two areas in which such restrictive citizenship practices caused most harm to Greek political development were colonization and conquest. When a Greek left home to join a colony, he forfeited citizenship in his native city. Instead of becoming an extension of a city, a colony became another independent polis. Likewise, when one Greek state conquered another, its restrictive citizenship practices,

eeling of exclusivity, and its unwillingness to surrender any of its
nomy contributed heavily to its reluctance and even inability to
rb the conquered city. As a result, conquest was seldom perma-
and did not break down the multiplicity of independent states.

Aristotle and Plato both astutely observed that the key to the
polis was *autarkia* or 'self-sufficiency', which they said should ideally
exist in everything, population, size and occupations. Aristotle
specified six necessary items for it: food supply, handicrafts, arms,
money supply, religion, and the legal system, with occupations
corresponding to these.

Self-sufficiency both permitted and prompted the development of
the polis in the Greek Dark Ages; but after the polis had developed to
a certain point its size and complexity militated against complete
independence. While trade and commerce were minimal and communities were separated by the geography of the land, they were
forced to become self-sufficient. But in time excess population compelled the establishment of colonies, which encouraged trade. In addition, the polis needed outside stimulation to avoid stagnation. But
outside contact created a new world order for which the polis was not
suited and to which it could not adapt politically.

Athens and Sparta represented the extremes of self-sufficiency.
Both extremes led to the failure of the polis. Sparta, almost totally
independent and isolated, decayed, while Athens, dependent on other
states, became incredibly vital and in order to survive had to create an
organization which superseded the polis. Since Sparta had ample land
to feed her population, she never became involved in colonization.
When the rest of Greece began to use coinage in the late seventh
century, Sparta did not follow suit, thus keeping herself independent
but isolating herself economically from the rest of Greece. Even when
Sparta conquered, she did not exploit her conquests, nor did she allow
them to interfere with her self-sufficiency. The result was degenera-
tion. In the seventh century she showed the same potential for cultural
growth as the rest of Greece. She supported poets such as Alcman,
and produced pottery as fine as that of any other state. But because she
kept out foreign influences and separated herself from the rest of
Greece stagnation set in. Industry and crafts were strangled; Sparta
became exclusively agricultural and gradually grew culturally barren.
Although militarily supreme because her citizens were professional
soldiers, her social fabric grew rotten and disintegrated, while her
citizen population rapidly declined. Though she was victorious in the

25–27 Seventh-century Sparta's cultural productions had been the equal of any in Greece, but the 'freezing' of the social structure after the Messenian Revolt was followed by the almost immediate wilting of native art. These examples date from the mid-sixth century B C, when the first signs of rigidity and a loss of vitality were beginning to appear: right, an abstract decoration on a mixing-bowl; below, a black-figure cup showing a boar-hunt and a bronze statuette of a girl with cymbals.

Peloponnesian War against Athens at the end of the fifth century, Sparta's collapse was even then imminent, since her inflexibility and isolation made her unable to adapt to the changing military tactics and social conditions of the early fourth century.

Athens faced her population problem in much the same way as Sparta, that is by extending her territory round the polis, rather than by colonization. Despite her initial lack of interest in colonization and commerce, her trade boomed in the sixth century, under the guidance of Solon and Peisistratus. As evidence of this we find Athenian pottery spread from the westernmost part of the Mediterranean to the shores of the Black Sea. At the same time, as olive and vine cultivation increased, the production of grain, a less profitable crop, fell. By the mid fifth century Athens was almost entirely dependent on the Black Sea region for grain. As Pericles, Athens' great statesman, said in the funeral oration referred to above, 'owing to the greatness of our city we draw from the produce of the whole earth, and it falls to us to enjoy the goods of foreign lands as readily as those of Attica herself'. Athens had lost her *autarkia* since she had become dependent on her vast trading empire. To continue as a polis she had to dominate the Aegean, and by doing this she created an organization which transcended the polis, the Athenian empire. She exchanged self-sufficiency for vitality. Art, literature and science flourished within her gates. Philosophers flocked to her – Gorgias of Leontini, Protagoras of Abdera, Anaxagoras of Clazomenae among others. Herodotus, the first Greek historian, came to her from Halicarnassus. Athens' greatness owed as much to the stimulus provided by outsiders as it did to the creative genius of her own citizens.

The polis was in many ways a place for the amateur. Self-sufficiency implies a lack of specialization and requires the citizen to be a Renaissance man – citizen, politician, soldier, farmer, craftsman. In fifth-century Athens a large percentage of the citizen population served in government posts of some kind at some time in their lives. All citizens were members of the assembly: to encourage them to attend its meetings a rope rubbed with red ochre was drawn across the market-place by Scythian bowmen, the Athenian police force, to drive the people to the assembly. The rope would leave a red stain on whomever it touched, thereby marking the tardy. The citizen also had to serve as a soldier or sailor, but this was only a part-time duty; campaigning seasons were short, since the soldier had to return to farm his land. Writers too were amateurs, as is well illustrated by

28 Mid-sixth-century Laconian cup showing Zeus and an eagle.

Aeschylus' request that the inscription on his tomb should read, not that he had won prizes in dramatic contests, but that he had served as a soldier at the battle of Salamis. The dramatist Sophocles served as a general in the campaign against Samos and was also a priest of the healing deity Amynos; he even turned his own house into a place of worship for Asclepius during the construction of the god's temple. Thucydides, the historian, was also a general. Solon, the great reformer, was an accomplished poet.

Amateurism even pervaded the law. Since there were no public prosecutors or judges, charges had to be brought by aggrieved individuals. A man could not hire a lawyer, but had to appear in court on his own behalf (though he could engage a speech-writer). Likewise priests were not usually from a professional class. The chief religious figure at Athens, for example, was the *archon basileus*, the 'king archon', an annually elected official. In some cases, however, as in the Eleusinian Mysteries, priesthoods were restricted to a particular clan or family, which probably resulted from those rites having originally been domestic or clan-centred. It was only towards the end of the fifth century that life began to be specialized. Philosophers such as Socrates advocated the doctrine of the expert: the man skilled in statecraft should run the state, just as the expert in the rearing of horses should manage horses. Warfare became too demanding for the part-time citizen soldiers, and mercenaries replaced them. Civilization in general was becoming too professional for the amateur. When the citizen of the polis no longer performed all the tasks of the state and began to specialize, he began to lose his intense loyalty to the polis and concentrated more on his own craft and his own life.

At the end of the fifth century we see the rise of individualism in all spheres of life. While Socrates was an active member of the state, Plato withdrew from active participation in it. The tragedians ceased to treat universal themes of the sort with which Aeschylus had dealt in the *Oresteia*, and Euripides and his contemporaries began to concentrate on individuals. Comedy became situation intrigue or parody instead of political satire. When the citizens of the polis rejected the sentiment of service to the polis in favour of service from the polis, its days were numbered as an effective political organization.

Plato and Aristotle saw the polis as the ideal for human existence because in such a social organization men could live the 'good life'. The small size which Plato and Aristotle considered necessary for the polis and their feeling that the polis should possess *autarkia* reflected the Greek belief that their particularism, which we condemn, was a virtue. There was an inherent contradiction between the theory of the polis as represented by Plato and Aristotle and the economic reality of Greece. Plato realized this inconsistency when he warned of the corrupting effect of commerce, which he correctly viewed as almost inevitably destroying self-sufficiency. Since every polis, except perhaps Sparta, was engaged in commerce to a greater or lesser degree from as early as the eighth century, *autarkia* in practice never really existed in Greece. The basis of the polis was believed to lie in *autarkia*; therefore domination of, or co-operation with, other states violated it. This may explain in part why, when one state conquered another, it often made little attempt to absorb its conquest. Thus in Greek thought there existed a fundamental and even theoretical contradiction between the polis as an idea and the polis as a realistic unit in the wider political scene. Their conception of the polis discouraged Greek states, with perhaps the exception of Athens, from consciously attempting either to modify their political system or to create a viable organization with which to replace it.

The polis was a political system created by a static agrarian society and was well suited to the needs of that society. With population increases and economic progress the size and the sphere of influence of the polis began to grow and it increasingly came into contact with other city states. But it could not overcome its own particularism, and thus the wars which followed this expansion were inevitable. The polis soon came to be too small a unit to allow for adequate self-defence. Trade and changing economic conditions shrank the world, and conflict with large military states like Persia meant that the individual polis could no longer protect itself in isolation. As a reaction to the Persian War, the Athenian empire and Peloponnesian League developed. This meant that no single unallied polis could continue its peaceful existence. The world had changed from one of small isolated states to one of great powers, but the polis did not change with it and so lost its effectiveness as a political unit.

Though it became less effective politically, however, it did not cease to be a cultural hot-house capable, in the fifth century, of producing one of the greatest creative eras in the world's history. The cultural life which flourished within its walls transcended the limitations of the polis as a political form. The splendid amateurism of Greek society produced creative heights in art, science, literature. Just as professionalism hurt the polis as a political unit, so it adversely affected its real creative spirit. The polis as the primary political and military unit of Greece ceased with the conquest of Greece by Philip of Macedon in 338 BC and by then the creative activity of fifth-century Greek culture was rapidly waning. No longer were poets and philosophers men of action, but rather, like Plato, they turned to contemplative life and to the theory rather than the practice of politics. The trend towards specialization produced the literary critics of the Alexandrian age, but no creative geniuses able to rival those to whom fifth-century Athens had given birth. Yet, despite the fact that the great period of the polis had passed, that it had ceased to be a viable political unit after the second century, the polis as a cultural concept, as a centre for art, literature and education, continued well into the Roman Empire. The creation of Greek cities throughout the world by Alexander spread the polis culture over most of the civilized world. For many centuries to come, the Greek city from the Punjab to Egypt to Marseilles remained spiritually a polis.

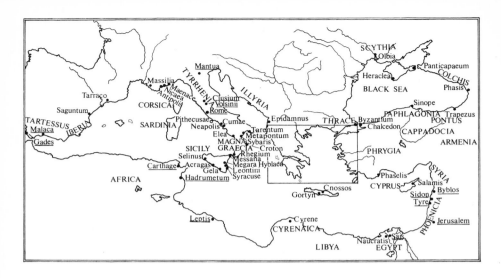

29, 30 The outreach of Greek colonization (cities underlined are non-Greek settlements).

III EXPANSION AND COLONIZATION

Colonization propagated the city state and made Greece wealthy and powerful; yet at the same time it planted the seeds of failure. Expansion, instead of creating a powerful united state, only further fragmented Greek society. In the eighth century twenty or thirty leading city states dominated Greece, and by the sixth century Greek civilization was distributed among hundreds of strong self-sufficient city states throughout the Mediterranean. A city state, as we have seen, founded a colony as an independent entity, not as a political extension of itself. This encouraged disunity, but at the same time it stimulated these colonies to grow strong and powerful, thereby increasing the aggregate power of Greek states. Of the numerous colonies planted by the Phoenicians throughout the Mediterranean, only a few, such as Carthage, grew mighty; but many Greek colonies became strong, often surpassing their founding city. Syracuse in Sicily came to dominate the surrounding region, as did Cyrene in North Africa, and Massilia in southern France. Dependent colonies could not have developed so rapidly or reached such a height of power.

Although to a limited extent Greeks could victoriously unite in the face of a mighty enemy such as Persia or Carthage, the internecine warfare between city states eventually so weakened them that in the fourth century they fell victim to Macedon, and in the second century to Rome. The polis produced a powerful and vital, but politically disorganized society. Those very factors which allowed the city states to spread and grow strong eventually led to their downfall.

GEOGRAPHICAL PATTERNS OF COLONIZATION
The polis society which reached its height in the sixth and fifth centuries BC was the ultimate successor to the Mycenaean. Struck by the violent upheavals of the thirteenth, twelfth and eleventh centuries BC, Greece recoiled. The flourishing Mycenaean civilization, which had sent its merchants, colonists and soldiers from Crete to Asia Minor and Sicily, collapsed. The Dark Ages descended on Greece.

Communication and trade between the remnants of Mycenaean civilization were reduced to a low ebb. Even the art of writing was all but lost, and civilization declined. Not until the eighth century did Greece emerge from her shell: a new method of writing was adopted; literature and art re-emerged and the great colonization movement began. The story of Greece's colonization period is one of the rise from the Dark Ages of ignorance, poverty and weakness to renewed heights of culture, power and wealth. In the eighth century Greeks moved east and west, in the seventh north and south, and in the sixth they consolidated their gains. From the eighth century, when she began her expansion, to the end of the sixth, Greece changed from a poor, agrarian, isolated, static society, confined to mainland Greece and the coast of Asia Minor, to a wealthy though fragmented power whose settlements extended from southern France to North Africa and from Egypt to southern Russia.

Plato compares the Greeks to frogs sitting on the edge of a great pond. This well describes the pattern of the Greek colonies, which were almost always located near the coast of the Mediterranean or the Black Sea. The Greeks had originally migrated into mainland Greece from the north through rough mountainous lands and there was no sufficient incentive for them to retrace their steps to these regions. Thus the Greeks turned to the sea as a natural route for colonization.

We can get an idea of the security and comfort the Greeks derived from the sea from an incident in the story of the escape of Xenophon and ten thousand Greek mercenaries from the midst of the hostile Persian empire. They had originally enlisted to fight in a civil war in Persia on the side of a viceroy named Cyrus against his brother, King Artaxerxes. At Cunaxa in 401 BC the two opposing forces had met, but though Cyrus and his Greeks prevailed, it was an empty victory, for Cyrus was killed in the fighting. The now unemployed Greek mercenaries began their long march home under the leadership of Xenophon, forced to fight for their lives at almost every step of the journey. One day, after an arduous trek, the vanguard of the troops had reached the top of a mountain when a great uproar was heard. To Xenophon and the rearguard it sounded as though an enemy was attacking. As each rank reached the top of the mountain, they too began to shout. Leaping on a horse, Xenophon rode ahead to investigate. In a moment he was close enough to distinguish the words the soldiers were shouting: 'The sea! The sea!' All the troops broke into a run and, when they reached the summit, embraced one another with

31 Late eighth-century Attic warship. The Greeks had been seafarers since early in their history, and until 400 BC, when the use of mercenary rowers became widespread, most maritime states depended on their own citizens to man their fleets, a dependence which could affect domestic policies.

tears in their eyes. It did not matter where or what sea the Greeks had reached. The sea meant orientation and a swift way home.

Much of the Mediterranean was not open to the Greeks. Few inroads were made in Egypt, the Levant, or the inland areas of northwest Asia Minor, which were already thickly settled. In North Africa and Spain the Greeks were blocked by Carthage and other Phoenician colonies, and in northern Italy by Etruria. However, they established colonies almost everywhere else on the Mediterranean.

The first thrust of the great colonization period was westward. Mainland Greek states such as Chalcis in Eretria sent colonies to Italy and Sicily. At the end of the eighth and beginning of the seventh century the Greeks descended in droves on southern Italy and the eastern coast of Sicily. The great sea power Corinth quickly joined in the race, founding Corcyra on the Adriatic and Syracuse in Sicily. The Achaeans, less interested in harbours, seized on the rich agricultural land at Metapontum, Croton and particularly Sybaris, where the land was so wealthy that the name 'sybarite' became synonymous with luxury. Then there was a hiatus until the last half of the seventh century, when the western portion of Sicily was settled, not by mainland Greeks, but by the cities of east Sicily – cities such as Megara Hyblaea, which founded Selinus, and Gela, which settled Acragas, a polis that was to grow into one of the most populous in the Mediterranean and to become renowned for its magnificent temples.

South Italy and Sicily became known as Magna Graecia – Great Greece. By the sixth and fifth centuries the cities of this area were larger, wealthier and more populous than those of mainland Greece.

47

32–35 Greek colonists exchanged the barren land and cramped conditions of their homelands for territories which sometimes grew rapidly to rival or surpass them in power and affluence. Above, the fertile plain of Sybaris in southern Italy; far left, pomegranate-picking in Sicily and agricultural prosperity symbolized on coins of Naxos (above), the first Greek colony to be settled in Sicily, and Metapontum.

36, 37 The colonials' sense of cultural inferiority to 'old Greece' often led to over-compensation. The two-storey 'Temple of Poseidon' at Paestum near Naples contrasts with the relatively unpretentious Theseum at Athens. The Paestum temple, however, shows provincialism in some of its details.

The Greeks who settled there became the *nouveaux riches*. Everything they built was 'bigger and better'. Their temples were larger and more ornate. Culturally, however, they lagged behind mainland Greece. Like colonial Americans, they were anxious for 'civilization' from the homeland. They imported creative men of all sorts, from artists to poets and philosophers, from Pindar, who wrote victory odes for the tyrant of Syracuse, to Plato, who tried to establish his ideal state under a philosopher king in Sicily. They regularly sent competitors in splendour to the Olympic Games, and if its contestants were victorious the entire city rejoiced in celebration. When a certain Exaenetus of Acragas was a victor in the ninety-second Olympiad, he was conducted into the city in a procession consisting of three hundred chariots, each drawn by two white horses. Two stories, though probably apocryphal, well portray how ravenous the Sicilian Greeks were for culture. In 413 BC survivors of the catastrophic Athenian campaign against Syracuse were given aid and shelter by the hostile Sicilian population in return for recitations of the verses of the playwright Euripides. Another story tells of a Caunian ship fleeing from pirates which once tried to sail into Syracuse but was forbidden entry until the sailors recited songs from Euripides.

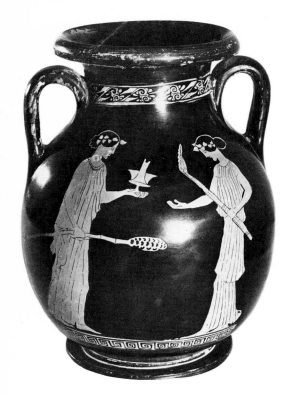

38 Vase from the Phocian colony of Massilia (Marseilles), founded on an excellent natural harbour in *c.* 600 BC, which became a prosperous and powerful centre for the diffusion of Greek culture and commerce.

Greeks even ventured out of the Mediterranean. About 638 BC a certain Colaeus of Samos was driven by a storm beyond the Pillars of Heracles (the Straits of Gibraltar) to Tartessus on the Atlantic coast of Spain. Since the area was unfrequented by Greeks, Colaeus found a virgin market and gained enormous profits from his voyage. Consequently, a colony was soon settled there to exploit the native market.

The great activity in the western Mediterranean caused a boom in trade, upon which the Phocians in particular capitalized. In their rapid progress in developing what was perhaps the most extensive trading empire in the Greek world, they settled trading colonies, which soon outgrew their original commercial function to become centres of Greek power. Such was the case with Massilia (Marseilles), which they founded about 600 BC. Massilia expanded swiftly, settling colonies of her own along the Riviera as far as Spain: Nicaea (Nice), Antipolis (Antibes) and Maenace (Monaco). Since, as we have seen, Spain was predominantly in Carthaginian and Phoenician hands, however, Greek expansion was blocked in that region and the trading empires of the Phocians and Carthaginians soon came to blows. In 535 BC the Phocians fought and defeated the combined Carthaginian and Etruscan fleets; but they suffered such heavy losses that Carthage was soon able to close the Straits of Gibraltar, destroy Tartessus and limit Greek trade in the far western Mediterranean.

Greeks had long been involved in the colonization of areas to the east of them. In the Late Mycenaean and sub-Mycenaean periods they had settled many colonies along the islands and western coast of Asia Minor (Aeolis and Ionia). During the Dark Ages they had lost almost all interest in colonization, but in the eighth century the colonial impulse re-emerged. Asia Minor, however, was no longer a fruitful area for colonization, especially in the Levant. That area was already heavily settled and colonization there was thus mostly precluded, except for a few trading centres such as Al Mina in north Syria. On the other hand the existing cities of Ionia and Aeolis could not expand inland into the heart of Asia Minor since they were hemmed in on that side by strong land powers such as the kingdom of Lydia. Consequently Greeks from both Asia Minor and the mainland sought less populous areas for development. At first their endeavours centred in the north Aegean on the Thracian coast and particularly around the Hellespont and Propontis (Sea of Marmara); next they expanded into the Black Sea region. Among the first colonization efforts were those of Megara, a small state of mainland Greece which established two cities on the Bosporus (Chalcedon and Byzantium) in order to dominate the Propontis and the entrance to the Black Sea. But the city which colonized most extensively was Ionian Miletus. Beginning with the foundation of Abydus on the Hellespont in the late seventh century, she embarked on the greatest colonial enterprise of the time, sending out about seventy colonies, primarily to the Black Sea region, the most important of which were Sinope and Trapezus on the south coast, and Olbia (near modern Odessa) on the north.

Although the Black Sea and northern colonies were settled in fertile areas and prospered, they never developed the culture or the power of the western colonies. They did, however, become the source of raw materials for mainland Greece. Iron, gold, fish, wood and leather were their major products, and in the fifth and fourth centuries Athens was largely dependent on these colonies for her grain supply. Although the area produced some brilliant men, such as Diogenes from Sinope, many of them went to mainland Greece and few returned. The area remained a cultural backwater.

COLONIAL CULTURE

39, 40 The colonies of 'Great Greece' (southern Italy and Sicily) emulated the culture and institutions of their founders but were soon producing artists, poets, scientists and philosophers whose work influenced the Greek world as a whole. Left, the theatre at Segesta, a non-Greek city in north-western Sicily which had nevertheless become thoroughly Hellenized by the fifth century BC. Right, an early artefact of the Greeks in Sicily – a cult image of an enthroned mother-goddess from Grammichele near Syracuse.

ΒΑΣΙΛΕΟΣΕΛΘΟΝΤΟΣΕΣΕΛΕΦΑΝΤΙΝΑΝΨΑΜΑΤΙΧΟ
ΤΑΥΤΑΕΓΡΑΨΑΝΤΟΙΣΥΝΨΑΜΜΑΤΙΧΟΙΤΟΙΘΕΟΚΛΟΣ
ΕΠΛΕΟΝΗΛΘΟΝΔΕΚΕΡΚΙΟΣΚΑΤΥΠΕΔΘΕΝΙΣΟΠΟΤΑΜΟΣ
ΑΝΙΗΛΟΓΛΟΣΟΣΟΕΤΕΠΟΤΑΣΙΜΤΟΑΙΓΥΠΤΙΟΣΔΕΡΜΑ
ΕΓΡΑΦΕΔΑΜΕΑΡΧΟΝΑΜΟΙΒΙΧΟΚΑΙΠΕΛΕΡΟΣΟΥΔΑ

41 Graffiti left by Greek mercenary soldiers on the leg of one of the colossal statues at Abu Simbel in Egypt. Such expeditions as these opened Greek eyes to a totally alien way of life.

Egypt prohibited the Greeks from settling colonies in her territory, with the notable exception of the trading colony of Naucratis in the Nile delta, founded in the sixth century. None the less, flourishing trade, tourism and mercenaries all brought the influence of Egypt back to Greece, particularly in the fields of art, monumental building and mathematics. According to Herodotus, Greeks in great numbers went to Egypt as tourists and traders, including Herodotus himself. Many went as mercenaries. One contingent of Greek soldiers left their 'calling cards' – initials and short graffiti on the monumental statues at Abu Simbel, seven hundred miles up the Nile. The longest reads: 'When King Psammetichos had come to Elephantine, this was written by those who sailed with Psammetichos, son of Theokles, who went as far upstream as they could – to Kerkis. Potasimto led the foreigners and Amasis the Egyptians. This was written by Archon, son of Amoibichos, and Pelekos, son of Eudamos.'

Greek colonization in North Africa was limited towards the east by Egypt and towards the west by Carthage. The powerful and important city of Cyrene was founded in about 670 BC between Egypt and Carthage, and it in turn sent out colonies to adjacent areas. But when at the end of the sixth century the Spartans tried to settle a colony to the west of Cyrene, perhaps in an attempt to outflank Carthage, the Carthaginians drove them out.

INDEPENDENT COLONIES
In the eighth century BC, when Greek colonization mushroomed, the main driving force was overpopulation. After the fall of Mycenaean civilization the population of Greece had declined, and the country as a whole became sparsely populated. The Dorian migrations into Greece increased the population, but not to any significant extent.

But the relative stability of the Dark Ages allowed numbers to swell unchecked, until by the eighth century overpopulation was critical. Two factors made the situation intolerable, the general poverty of Greek soil and the continual subdividing of land. The poorness of the land made it impossible for most city states to feed their growing populations. In most states, moreover, no rule of primogeniture existed. When a man died, instead of his eldest son inheriting the land, with the younger sons entering other professions and trades, land was divided among all the sons. The eighth-century poet Hesiod gives us an insight into the economic problems of his time. In his verses he complains that the greedy nobles have seized the best lands and the poor farmers have been left with stony and barren soil. Further, he bewails his troubles with his brother Perses, who gained more than his share of their father's property. Hesiod cautions the farmer to have only one son if he wishes to prosper. The continual subdivision of the land rapidly produced lots inadequate in size for effective farming. Hungry bellies drove Greeks to the colonies, a motivation well shown by the rapacity of the early colonists in seizing fertile areas.

The situation on the island of Thera illustrates the problem and an attempted solution. Though the land of the island was fertile, it was very limited in area and according to Herodotus the Theraeans, when

42 Statuette of a ploughman and his team from Boeotia, seventh century BC. Population pressures also stimulated an improvement in agricultural methods during the classical period: different soil types were distinguished, for instance, and crop rotation introduced.

faced with drought and accompanying crop failure at the end of the seventh century, sent colonists 'taking by lot one of every pair of brothers'. So severe was the situation that the penalty for failing to go when chosen was death. At first unsuccessful in their venture, the colonists attempted to return. But as they tried to land the Theraeans showered them with arrows and drove them off. The purpose of the colony was to relieve population pressure; that of conscripting one heir from each household to halt or at least arrest the rate at which land was being subdivided.

Trade was inextricably tied to colonization, since each stimulated the other. To a degree trade antedates the great colonial period. One of the earliest colonies, that at Al Mina in Syria on the mouth of the Orontes (today in Turkey), dates from the beginning of the eighth century and was specifically a trading centre. When Chalcis and Eretria founded the first colony in the west, they chose the site of Pithecusae (modern Ischia) in the Bay of Naples, a position ideal for trading purposes. A settlement on the mainland at Cumae followed next, but the rich agricultural lands nearby were passed over. Pithecusae and Cumae may have been established as trading colonies to acquire from Etruria the valuable metals which Greece, a country poor in minerals, sorely needed. Once Greeks had become familiar with the area through the activities of traders, the most fertile coastal land in eastern Sicily and southern Italy was colonized for agriculture. Many of these later colonies, for whatever reason they may originally have been settled, became important markets. Traders brought grain, foodstuffs and metals back to mainland Greece, and exported manufactured goods. As trade increased in scope, new areas were opened where further colonies might be founded.

Many factors prompted the foundation of colonies as independent political units. In the early period of colonization, in the eighth century, states were primarily concerned with solving their narrow problems of population pressure, rather than with building colonial empires. They wanted to rid themselves of excess population and to stabilize their own situations, as in the case of Cyrene. It did not matter to the founding cities whether they exercised strict political control over their colonies. The feeling of exclusiveness in the polis, the necessity of owning land in order to be a citizen, and the need to be on the spot, to be able to vote in the assemblies and to take a proper part in the life of the tribe – duties which an absent colonist could not perform – all encouraged autonomous colonies.

43 The Temple of Concord at Acragas in Sicily: Empedocles said of his fellow townsmen, 'The people of Acragas revel as if they were going to die tomorrow and build as if they were going to live for ever.'

Colonies were founded as acts of state policy, as political and religious institutions in the image of the mother city. Divine sanction, often from the Oracle at Delphi, was sought. As a result many colonies claimed Apollo as their founder, and Delphi, a centre for the worship of Apollo, became the arbiter in some colonial disputes. An official decree regulating the colony was drawn up. The foundation decree of Naupactus may serve as a representative example:

The colony at Naupactus is to be established on the following terms. The Hypocnemidian Locrian, when he becomes a Naupactian, shall, being a Naupactian, have the right, when present, to sacrifice and obtain a share of the sacrifice, in the places where a stranger is permitted by sacred law, if he so wish. If he so wish he shall make offerings and receive a share both in the sacrifices of the people and in those of the societies, he and his family for ever. The colonists of the Hypocnemidian Locrians shall not pay tax among the Hypocnemidian Locrians until one of them becomes again a Hypocnemidian Locrian. If the colonist wishes to return, it shall be allowed without payment of fees so long as he leaves for the household a grown son or brother. If the Hypocnemidian Locrians are driven out of Naupactus by force, they shall be permitted to return, each to his previous home, without entry fees. They shall pay no tax except in common with the West Locrians.

1 The colonists to Naupactus are to take an oath not to secede voluntarily from the Opuntians by any means or device whatever. If they wish it shall be permitted, thirty years after the swearing of the oath, for one hundred men from the Naupactians to administer the oath to the Opuntians, and from the Opuntians, to the Naupactians.

2 Whoever of the colonists defaults in his tax payments in Naupactus shall be excluded from the Locrians until he pays his lawful dues to the Naupactians.

3 If the colonist have no successors in his house, nor heir among the colonists in Naupactus, the next of kin among the Hypocnemidian Locrians shall inherit, wherever he may come from among the Locrians, so long as he comes in person, whether man or boy, within three months. But otherwise the laws of Naupactus shall be applied.

4 If the colonist return from Naupactus to the Hypocnemidian Locrians he shall have it proclaimed in the market-place at Naupactus, and among the Hypocnemidian Locrians he shall have it announced in the market-place of his city of origin.

5 Whenever a member of the Percothariae and Mysacheis himself becomes a Naupactian, his property in Naupactus shall also be subject to the laws of Naupactus. But his property among the Hypocnemidian Locrians shall be subject to the laws of the Hypocnemidian Locrians, as the laws of the Hypocnemidian Locrian city of each individual stand. But if one of the Percothariae and Mysacheis return under the laws relating to the colonists, he shall be subject to his own laws, each in his city.

6 If the settler in Naupactus shall have brothers, as the law stands in each city of the Hypocnemidian Locrians, if the brother dies the colonist shall take possession of the property, that is shall possess his due share.

7 The colonists to Naupactus shall have precedence in bringing suits before the judges; the Hypocnemidian Locrian shall bring suits and answer suits against himself in Opus on the same day. Those who are the magistrates of the year shall appoint a *prostates* for the colonist from the Locrians, and from the colonists for the Locrian.

8 Whoever of the colonists to Naupactus leaves behind a father and leaves his property with his father, shall be allowed, when the father dies, to recover his share.

9 Whoever shall violate these decisions by any means or device whatever, except after a decree both of the assembly of the Thousand at Opus and the assembly of the colonists at Naupactus, shall be outlawed and his property shall be confiscated. The magistrate shall grant a trial to the accuser within thirty days, if thirty days of his magistracy are left. If he does not grant a trial to the accuser, he shall be outlawed and his property confiscated, his land together with his servants. They are to swear the oath prescribed by law. The votes are to be cast into an urn. And the statute for the Hypocnemidian Locrians is to be valid in the same way for the settlers from Chaleum with Antiphatas. (tr. A.J. Graham)

The state also appointed a foundation official, called an *oikistes*, as the temporary leader of the colony.

The colonist's loss of citizenship in his native city indicates most clearly that colonies were founded and intended as independent entities. Light is thrown on the question of citizenship by the surviving official decrees which formally provided for the foundation of colonies. The mid–fifth–century foundation decree of Naupactus, quoted above, states that a colonist becomes a Naupactian and ceases to be a citizen of

Hypocnemidian Locris. Locris founded Naupactus for political reasons rather than because of overpopulation, and was forced to offer inducements to people to become colonists. This is evidenced by the generous provisions of the foundation decree. A colonist could regain citizenship in Locris if he left behind a grown son or brother in Naupactus, or if he were compelled by necessity to return. The decree also implies that a colonist could return if these conditions were not fulfilled, though a penalty would then be payable. To protect the colony, colonists were discouraged from returning home. Rights of inheritance and kinship, however, persisted between the two cities. According to a fourth-century BC copy of Cyrene's foundation charter, a colonist would become a citizen of Cyrene and would lose all claim of citizenship in Thera unless the Theraeans neglected to aid the colony, or the colony was failing, or the colonists returned within five years. In practice, however, return might be difficult or impossible, as Herodotus describes.

Miletus, the most prolific among colonizing cities, seems to have pursued a more flexible policy with regard to citizenship rights in the colony and the mother city. This was, at least, apparently the practice with certain colonies, such as Olbia, in the Black Sea region. Unfortunately the evidence in this case is late, dating from the fourth century, but it may be indicative of conditions in the sixth and fifth centuries. Milesians could choose to become citizens of Olbia and Olbians could claim the same privilege in Miletus. In each case, however, full citizenship in one required the relinquishing of full citizenship in the other. But another option was open to the Milesian or Olbian. He could maintain citizenship in one state and at the same time claim limited rights in the other, such as exemption from taxes and equality with citizens in religious matters, though he would not be entitled to hold public office. In granting these unusual rights, Miletus may have been influenced by the commercial purposes her colonies were meant to serve. Despite Miletus' liberality, the concept that the colonist might simultaneously be a full citizen of the mother city existed neither in Miletus nor almost anywhere else.

Reciprocal citizenship was not the normal institution in colonization. The usual pattern seems to have been that of Cyrene, and generally the right of return was at most permitted only to the first settlers, as at Naupactus. The colonists did not have any automatic or permanent right to citizenship in the mother city once they had left. However, the latter could and did send more than one wave of colonists.

44 Laconian cup showing trade with Cyrene, the Theraean colony in North Africa. King Arcesilas II of Cyrene supervises the weighing out and storing of wool (or possibly silphium, his city's main product).

Though a colony was politically independent of its mother city, there were generally strong ties between them. When a colony sent out a colony of its own it often, even after many years of independence, invited its mother city to provide the *oikistes*. The family, tribal and kinship organizations on which the original city was based persisted in the colony, and colonists usually took fire from the sacred hearth of the mother city to kindle their own sacred hearth. At the end of the fifth century, on the eve of the Peloponnesian War, the Corinthians sought a pretext for war by charging their colonists the Corcyreans with neglecting their religious obligations to their mother city. Because of the close ties between mother city and colony, war between the two was regarded as shameful, although in the case of Corinth and Corcyra a particularly fierce and persistent struggle did in fact ensue. Usually the mother city regarded herself as the protector of her colony. For example, according to Xenophon, after the Athenians had been defeated by Sparta in the Peloponnesian War their greatest fear was that the Spartans would kill them in retribution for Athens' mass execution of the men of Melos, which was a Spartan colony.

Colonial attitudes in Cyrene are well exemplified in two odes of Pindar, *Pythian* 4 and *Pythian* 9. Both poems are attempts to legitimize the Greek origins of the colony through foundation myths. In *Pythian* 4 the beginnings of the colony are traced first to Battus, and then further back to Mycenaean times, to Euphemus, one of the heroes who accompanied Jason and the Argonauts in the search for the Golden Fleece. In *Pythian* 9, written to celebrate the victory of Telesicrates of Cyrene in the foot-race in full armour at the Pythian Games of 474 BC, Pindar goes one step beyond the Argonauts and traces the origins of Cyrene to the gods themselves, the mating of Apollo with Cyrene, daughter of Hypseus, the ruler of the Lapithae. The Cyreneans were conscious of their kinship relations with Thera and Sparta, and emphasized their descent from the Argonauts. The name 'Jason was probably not uncommon, which is suggested by the fact that it occasionally occurs as the magistrate's name on some of their coins. Through the foundation myths, the Cyreneans had transformed and hallowed the origins of their colony: from being a group largely conscripted in time of famine and dispatched to relieve excess population, they became the descendants of one of the Argonauts, and were thus able to view their city as divinely inspired in its origins and guided by fate.

45, 46 Left, coin of Cyrene showing the head of Zeus Ammon, a Hellenized version of the Egyptian Amon-Ra whose cult exemplifies the cultural fusion common between Greek colonists and surrounding native peoples. Right, coin of Corinth showing Pegasus and the ancient letter 'koppa'; colonies under Corinthian control displayed their dependence on their mother city by minting coins with the same motif, merely substituting the initial letter of their own city for the koppa.

IMPERIAL COLONIES

Not until population pressures were somewhat eased in the late seventh century did states begin to see in colonization a means of extending political power. Although their aims changed, however, their patterns of colonization remained the same, and they were thus faced with the new task of preventing the colonies from becoming totally autonomous states. The Greek tyrants tried to solve this problem by two methods, by military domination and by the sending of their own sons, relatives or close allies as *oikistai* and governors of the colonies. These men, they hoped, could be relied upon to keep the colony subservient, or at least loyal. Corinth followed the same practice during her period of rule by tyrants, but relied mainly on naval power to dominate her colonies. These methods, however, failed to offset the natural tendency towards autonomy, a tendency inherent in the political structure of the colony.

The activities of the tyrants of Corinth and Athens illustrate the use of relatives, friends and allies as a means of colonial domination. Cypselus, tyrant of Corinth, dispatched his sons as *oikistai* to found Leucas, Ambracia and Anactorium. Potidaea had as its *oikistes*

Evagoras, a son of Periander, a later tyrant of Corinth. Another son of Periander was involved in Corcyra. When he was killed by the Corcyreans, Periander invaded and crushed the dissidents with his troops, and installed his nephew as the ruler of the polis. As a further punishment, Periander took three hundred boys, the sons of leading men of the city, and sent them to Sardis in Lydia with the intention of having them castrated. Probably he intended to have them sold as eunuchs. Fortunately for the boys, however, Greeks from the island of Samos rescued them in time. In the case of Athens, the tyrant Peisistratus settled the colony of Sigeum under his son Hegesistratus in about 530 BC. Miltiades the elder, although a rival of Peisistratus, was supported by the tyrant in his occupation of the Thracian Chersonese in the mid-sixth century. Towards the end of the sixth century the younger Miltiades was sent out by Peisistratus' son Hippias to rule the colony. To a limited extent the tyrants in Corinth and Athens were thus able to use colonies for imperial aims, though the tyrants in other states did not, as a rule, do so.

Of all the city states Corinth came the closest to establishing a colonial empire. She preserved a tight relationship with her colonies and held political supremacy to a limited degree. The ease with which Corinth moved new settlers into her colonies of Anactorium and Epidamnus in 432/431 BC suggests that Corinthians could take up citizenship in these colonies, although the colonists could not easily return to Corinth. The colonists managed their own foreign policy so long as no conflict arose with respect to Corinth's interests. Corinth, for her part, supported these cities in time of trouble and had close commercial ties with them. Nevertheless, despite her desire to control her colonies, Corinth followed the same practice as other Greek states in establishing her settlements as independent entities. This encouraged separation, not union. Sea power, however, enabled her to dominate her lesser colonies and to this degree she succeeded in forming a colonial empire. But she could not maintain much influence over the two colonies which were the largest and most powerful militarily and politically – Corcyra and Syracuse.

Corcyra and Syracuse were established in the late eighth century, before the period of the tyrants, not as politically dependent colonies, but as outlets for excess population. Partly for this reason, and partly because of their great distance from Corinth, the mother city initially made little attempt to control them, and they became strong and autonomous. Corcyra was hostile to Corinth almost from the moment of her foundation. She grew in power so rapidly that by 664 she was contesting Corinth's power in north-west Greece. In that year colony and mother city fought a sea battle. By the late seventh century, however, relations had become amicable. About 600 BC, while Periander was tyrant in Corinth, Corcyra again fell under Corinthian influence. Then, during the sixth century, she regained her independence and became embroiled in further disputes with Corinth over the colonies of Leucas, Anactorium and Epidamnus. In 433 BC the first incident of the Peloponnesian War was triggered off when Epidamnus appealed in vain to her mother city, Corcyra, for aid against her exiled oligarchs and native tribes, who were attacking her. Epidamnus then turned to the Corinthians, who agreed to aid her, precipitating an armed conflict between Corcyra and Corinth in which Athens took the part of Corcyra and earned Corinth's active hostility.

Syracuse grew more slowly than Corcyra, but ultimately became more powerful and rose to be the leading state in Sicily. Relations between Syracuse and her mother city remained cordial throughout her history and ties were always close. When Hippocrates of Gela defeated Syracuse in 492 BC, the Corinthians intervened to mediate in the dispute on Syracuse's behalf. When Athens attacked Syracuse in 415 BC, Corinth gave her colony full support (albeit motivated less by a sense of obligation to her colony than by enmity to Athens). In 344 BC, at the request of the Syracusan aristocrats, the general Timoleon was sent from Corinth to aid them against their tyrant.

As large and powerful states, Corcyra and Syracuse for the most part defended their independence and remained outside Corinth's hegemony. Because of her method of founding colonies, Corinth was able to control only weaker settlements, thus limiting the success of her effort to extend political power through this means. Had Corinth created her colonies as an integral part of her state and thereby formed a united power with the combined wealth and might of Syracuse and Corcyra, she might have emerged as the leading power in Greece, as later Athens did through her empire and Sparta through the Peloponnesian League.

Unlike other Greek cities in the eighth and seventh centuries, Athens was not compelled by circumstances to found new cities. Instead she chose to solve her population problem by utilizing the resources of Attica..Although the land was poor, it was sufficient in area to feed the state. Her colonies of the tyrant period, such as Chersonese and Sigeum, were, like those of Corinth, founded for imperialistic motives. After the Persian War in the early fifth century Athens initiated a great wave of expansion and transformed the Delian League, which had been created to fight Persia, into the Athenian empire. Consequently, in her colonizing activities during the fifth century, which were stimulated mainly by the desire to secure and expand her empire, Athens was reluctant to establish colonies which might break away from her: she had already encountered difficulty with cities in her empire which had attempted revolt. Recognizing the tendency of the normal colony to seek autonomy, the Athenians went one step further than the institution of reciprocal rights of citizenship practised by Miletus with some of her colonies and devised a hybrid, the 'cleruchy' system. A cleruchy was a settlement of Athenian citizens (called 'cleruchs' because they were assigned a *kleros* or 'lot') who went out to a colony, but remained citizens of Athens. In effect, this type of settlement became an extension of the Athenian state abroad. A very small number of cleruchs remained in Athens as absentee land-owners, although, like the others, they were assigned lots in the cleruchies. All cleruchs retained the rights, privileges and obligations of Athenian citizens, such as liability to general military service and to war taxes. But since cleruchies were composed of Athenian citizens, they were exempted from the tribute paid by other members of the Athenian empire.

Cleruchies were sent out for three purposes: to found a city on a new site; to replace an expelled or executed population; or to re-inforce an existing settlement. Often after a city in the empire had revolted Athens sent in cleruchs to settle a portion of the land of the defeated state, at the same time reducing the assessed tribute to compensate for the confiscated land. The cleruchs served as a stabilizing element in the city, and as a means through which Athens exercised her hegemony. This was the case at Naxos, for example, after the revolt of 470 BC. At Melos in 416 BC the Athenians executed the entire male population, sold the women and children into slavery and settled the island with cleruchs. Similarly, large numbers of cleruchs were sent to Aegina and Hestiaea after the native Greek inhabitants had been expelled. In Lemnos in the late fifth century we find two groups of Athenians, cleruchs and non-cleruch colonists, co-existing on the island. Apparently the former were new colonists. This did not immediately affect the position of the earlier Athenian colonists, but by the fourth century all the settlers on Lemnos had achieved the status of cleruchs.

The cleruchy system proved an effective means of extending Athenian power while avoiding the problems encountered in the more usual form of colony. Nevertheless, Athens did not pursue this system consistently, perhaps because of a reluctance on the part of her citizens to go too far afield. Many cleruchies, such as at Chalcis and Aegina, were geographically close to Athens. However, her failure to employ the cleruchy system everywhere may well have been caused by Athens' restrictive citizenship practices at home. In the mid-fifth century Athens had only about thirty thousand to forty thousand adult male citizens, a number insufficient to expand her empire through the widespread use of the cleruchy system. She had found only a partial answer.

Athens was therefore forced to establish colonies of the normal Greek pattern, such as Brea, Thurii and Amphipolis. Brea was settled in the mid-fifth century to shore up Athenian military power on the northern Aegean coast, its location being chosen for strategic considerations. Democlides, an Athenian official, was dispatched to organize the new town, but he performed his function as an agent of Athens rather than as a traditional *oikistes*, and once his task was accomplished he returned home to Athens. Brea was a small colony, however, and seems to have disappeared fairly soon after its foundation; most likely it was absorbed into the new colony of Amphipolis, settled nearby.

The most important of the regular colonies of this period were Thurii and Amphipolis, which were probably established for imperialistic motives. Athens encountered considerable problems with them. In 437/436 BC Amphipolis, like Brea, was founded on the northern Aegean coast to strengthen Athenian power in that area. Hagnon, a leading military and political figure in Athens, went out as the *oikistes*, set up a democratic constitution and then left the city. The large population necessary for the safety of a city in that region precluded Athens from founding a cleruchy, and the origin of the settlers was mixed, with many coming from neighbouring Argilus. Amphipolis became the operating headquarters of two Athenian generals, and the defence and control of the city was in Athenian hands. And yet, because they were not Athenians either in kinship or in citizenship, most of the people of Amphipolis felt little loyalty to Athens. Certain elements were ready to betray the city to the Spartan general Brasidas during the Peloponnesian War and at one point the Amphipolitans were prepared to fight against Athens. Later, after Sparta had gained control of the city, they repudiated their connection with Athens and adopted Brasidas as their *oikistes*.

Thurii, whose foundation was sponsored by Pericles, was settled in 444 BC in southern Italy, near the former site of Sybaris which had been destroyed in 510 BC. Because Athens had an insufficient number of colonists at her disposal for a strong settlement, Pericles invited any Greek to join the colony. This was an unusual situation, since normally, if a foreigner came to a colony, he was not admitted to citizenship, but became a 'metic'. Any free man who came to Thurii, however, could become a full citizen and member of the colony. Later Greeks, especially in the fourth century, romanticized Thurii as the first effort towards Panhellenism: Herodotus settled there; according to some ancient sources, the philosopher Protagoras drew up its law codes; Hippodamus the town-planner reputedly laid out the city; Cleandridas, an exiled Spartan leader, joined the colony. Athens' motive, however, was probably to secure a foothold in the West through this city, a goal which was only partially successful. In 434/433 BC fighting broke out between the Peloponnesian and Athenian citizens over which was their mother city and who was their *oikistes*. Asked to mediate, the Oracle of Apollo at Delphi solved the problem by declaring Apollo the *oikistes*. This represented a setback for Athens, but the Athenian element did remain in power until the defeat of Athens in Sicily in 413 BC. In 412 BC Thurii expelled many citizens for pro-Athenian sympathies, and allied herself with the Peloponnesians. The pattern emerges that Athens did not have the resources to use the cleruchy system effectively, nor to found large colonies, while colonies of mixed origin proved untenable for her purposes.

THE IMPACT OF COLONIZATION
The colonization movement was, on the whole, a tremendous success. Greek power was spread throughout the Mediterranean, and mainland Greece reaped many benefits. Colonization brought wealth back to the homeland: metals once rare now came from the East and the West; grain and foodstuffs were shipped home. This enabled Greece to industrialize, to produce pottery and metalwork which could be sent to the colonies. New prosperity came to the states, though it was not spread to all levels of society, and with it populations increased still further. Population pressures were not, therefore, completely alleviated by colonization, but the subdividing of land was slowed and new trades and professions were created.

The great age of colonization brought Greek culture to numerous places in the Mediterranean and Black Sea. The colonies remained Greek. Their strength lay in their exclusiveness, their conviction that they were independent political centres, and that they were better than the 'barbarians' who lived about them. Their attitude and the constant trade and commerce with mainland Greece helped them to retain their cultural identity. The western Greeks were very conscious of their Hellenism, and, especially when they intermarried, they strove to retain their identity. On the fringes of colonial areas the Greeks were slightly more influenced by the natives, as in Cyrene and the Crimea, but they nevertheless remained thoroughly Greek.

The Greek colonies exercised an overwhelming influence on native populations. Etruscan civilization was heavily in their debt. Roman culture began under the stimulus of Greek cities in southern Italy, and after Rome's conquest of these areas the Hellenic spirit with its art, literature, philosophy and science inundated Rome. Educated Romans in later centuries became fluent in the Greek language and the acceptance of things Greek was to become so widespread that the poet Horace described the Hellenic impact with the words, 'Greece, though conquered, conquered its wild vanquisher [Rome].' Greeks introduced oil and the vine into southern France and left many mute testaments to their presence. As far north and west as Vix in central France, in a princess's tomb, a great bronze crater of probable Peloponnesian origin, dating from the sixth century, was unearthed. In southern Russia gold and silver artefacts were discovered in Scythian royal tombs, products of Greek artists of the area who fused native themes with Hellenic craftsmanship.

Colonies were largely unsuccessful as an avenue for extending political power, primarily because they were never intended to perform this function. They were founded as separate city states and separate city states they remained. Athens recognized the shortcomings of the system when, in furtherance of her own ambitions, she turned towards imperialistic expansion and applied ingenuity in devising the cleruchy to overcome the problem of local autonomy. But this revolutionary solution proved only partially successful, as we have seen.

Thus no Greek polis was able to prevent the natural tendency towards the fragmentation of the Greek world, which the establishment of colonies only served ultimately to exacerbate. The fundamental problem of disunity had not been overcome.

IV GREEK IMPERIALISM

A state may control its conquests by various means – legal, constitutional, religious, economic and military. But whatever methods are employed, one of its primary tasks is to create a cohesive organization. The Romans proved the efficacy of granting citizenship as a means of ensuring loyalty and cohesion. After conquering a nearby tribe, they usually made its members half-citizens and later full citizens. Rome's policy was one of the assimilation and incorporation of conquered states into the Roman polity. Such a concept was totally alien to the Greek city states. Their narrow views in this regard made it almost unthinkable for them to grant citizenship to the conquered in the fifth century. Athens dealt with the problem of uniting her empire better than most, especially since she was almost unique in grasping the importance of citizenship as a unifying element. On the other hand, Sparta's restrictive citizenship practices created for her both internal weakness and enormous difficulty in absorbing conquered peoples. Thus Aristotle observed that the cult of military prowess leads to victory unaccompanied by any comprehension of what to do with it.

THE SPARTAN EXPERIMENT

Sparta was probably already the largest town of the region of Laconia in the ninth century when she began her period of great expansion. She extended her rule first northwards, then southwards, conquering neighbouring towns such as Amyclae. In the middle of the eighth century, having solidified her position in the upper Eurotas valley, she subdued nearby Messenia.

Sparta absorbed these conquests in a way which dictated much of her future history. Outside Sparta herself, the vanquished population was divided into two groups, the *perioikoi* ('those who dwell round about') and the helots. The *perioikos* was a full citizen in his own town with no personal obligation to Sparta, though he was subject to Spartan magistrates. His town, however, was autonomous only in local matters and had to provide troops for Sparta. (This was in marked

71

48 Black-figure cup from Rhodes showing a charging hoplite whose shield clearly demonstrates the characteristic hoplite grip: the soldier inserted his arm through the central ring and clasped a handle near the edge.

contrast to Athens, where, upon the unification of Attica, a common citizenship was created.) In most of conquered Messenia and parts of Laconia, the populace were reduced to helotry. A helot was much like a feudal serf, but unlike a serf he belonged to the state and was assigned to a master who was usually absent. Though the Spartans tied the helot to the land, they seldom interfered with him, so long as he was productive. Yet the helots had no civil rights and could be executed without trial by the Spartans, as indeed they often arbitrarily were. These murders were institutionalized by an official organization called the *krypteia*, literally 'secret service'. Plutarch tells us that from time to time the magistrates sent young warriors equipped with daggers out into the countryside. During the day they hid, but at night they would swoop down on to the highways and kill every helot they could catch. At times they even went through the fields murdering the sturdiest helots. Thucydides records a gruesome incident when the Spartans announced that all helots who claimed to have rendered Sparta the best service in war should be set apart to be freed. They were in fact only testing to find out who claimed the right of freedom, since they felt these would be the most high-spirited and most likely to attack their masters. Two thousand helots had wreaths set on their heads as tokens of emancipation and in procession they visited the temples of the gods. Then they all disappeared, quietly murdered. It was said that 'in Sparta the free man is more a free man than anywhere else in the world, and the slave more a slave'.

The helots retained a strong group identity, since they were probably Ionian in origin – while the Spartans were Dorian – although by the fifth century their language and customs had clearly been assimilated to those of their oppressors. They vastly outnumbered the Spartans and were ever ready to revolt, especially in Messenia. Spartan anxiety over the threat of helot uprisings was not unfounded, as several major revolts demonstrated.

During the eighth century, other Greek states expanded through the foundation of colonies, which stimulated trade. This in turn required manufactured goods and encouraged the development of a commercial class. Sparta, however, by her conquest of Messenia, had gained a substantial amount of land and wealth, a development which turned her interests away from overseas expansion, although she did occasionally establish colonies during her history. She committed herself to an agricultural future and a polarized society of master and helot. In acquiring and developing her conquests Sparta created a

49 Cup from Sparta showing warriors bearing away their dead – a vivid expression of the austere military ethic that dominated Spartan life.

virtual slave-labour force and to keep this force in check her society was impelled to become increasingly militaristic. These factors prevented the development of a real commercial class, except in the case of a few *perioikoi*, and generated an atmosphere of suspicion and strong conservatism.

The colonization and industrialization of Greece in the eighth century, along with the introduction of the hoplite at the beginning of the seventh, prompted tyranny in many Greek states. In other Greek states the tyrants emerged as champions of both the hoplites and the commercial class, but, since Sparta lacked the latter, the struggle there took place only between aristocrat and hoplite. Instead of tyranny and civil war a compromise, embodied in a new 'constitution', was reached between the two groups. This code was called the 'Lycurgan Constitution' since its origin was ascribed to a quasi-historical figure called Lycurgus. Whether or not Lycurgus ever existed, it is certain that the development of the system extended over a long period, with the main framework probably dating to the early seventh century. Parts of it, for example the prohibition against silver currency, must be of a later date, since such a provision could not have existed before the introduction of silver money into Greece in the late seventh century. Part of the constitution was called the 'Great Rhetra', which Plutarch tells us was an oracle obtained from Delphi by Lycurgus. Under the Lycurgan constitution the hoplites were known as 'equals', which may suggest that they had been unequal before it. Formal qualification for citizenship was henceforth based on a Spartan's ability to contribute to the *syssition*, or common table. At birth each citizen was assigned a *kleros*, or 'lot' of inalienable land. It was in the state's interest that this land be so encumbered since, were the land to be sold, the Spartan would not be able to contribute to the common table and the state would thus be deprived of both a citizen and a soldier. Lycurgus' system provided for the *agoge*, a programme of military training in which a Spartan was enrolled from the ages of seven to twenty. At twenty the Spartan joined the class of *eirenes*, as a member of which he gained certain citizenship rights and was liable for military service. Finally, at the age of thirty, he was admitted to the assembly and full legal privileges, including the right to marry.

Given this system with a subject population and severely restricted citizenship, it would have been extremely difficult for Sparta to

50–53 The need to create unities larger than the city state led to the formation of federations which claimed to preserve each member's freedom. Not all were as large, powerful or potentially strife-torn as the Peloponnesian and Delian Leagues. Right, coins of the Euboean League founded after the island's revolt from Athens in 411 BC and the Chalcidian League.

produce enough soldiers to subdue another state in the way that she had Messenia. To integrate another large city into her rigidly arranged class structure would have been an even more arduous task. This left federation as her natural means of expansion.

At the end of the sixth century the Peloponnesian League, a defensive-offensive military alliance between Sparta and other Peloponnesian states, came into existence. (Members of the League could, however, fight against one another, so long as the League as a whole was not at war.) It was an unequal alliance, with Sparta at the head. In contrast to some of the Hellenistic federated leagues, no common citizenship existed, but each man remained a citizen of his own polis. In the Peloponnesian League and others of this type the leading state tended to gain increasing power at the expense of the other members. The final result was a loosely unified group, dominated by the strongest. Resignation from the League became impossible, except by force. Though the decision of the Spartan assembly was binding on the League, the advisory opinion of League delegates was usually heeded by Sparta. Unlike the Athenian-dominated Delian League, the Peloponnesian possessed no formal organization and there were no officials. This type of organization produced no unity among its members: Sparta's inability to persuade her allies to abide by the terms of the Peace of Nicias in 421 BC is but one example of this. Within a few years of the defeat of their common enemy, Athens, in the Peloponnesian War, Sparta was herself at war with the strongest members of the League.

In the course of her conquest of other states, Sparta showed a singular inability to absorb or integrate her conquests. Either she left states as virtually autonomous members of the Peloponnesian League or she regulated them strictly through military garrisons and the support of oppressive pro-Spartan oligarchies. This failure is only partially explained by her ultra-conservative foreign policy.

At the end of the sixth century, having achieved dominance in the Peleponnese, Sparta undertook one of her first military actions outside it in the expulsion of the tyrant Hippias from Athens. In 510 BC the Alcmaeonids, an aristocratic clan which had been exiled from Athens, requested Spartan help against Hippias. Seizing this opportunity to extend her influence over Athens, an ally of her enemy Argos, Sparta readily acceded to the invitation. But once Hippias had been driven into exile, Sparta swiftly deserted the Alcmaeonid leader Cleisthenes, who had democratic tendencies, in favour of Isagoras, an oligarch.

54 Greek hoplite fighting with an Asiatic, probably a member of the Persian Army. The Greek's nudity is an artistic convention designed to distinguish his Greekness from his barbarian opponent.

In 508 BC she unsuccessfully sent troops to Athens to support Isagoras. In a complete *volte-face*, Cleomenes, the Spartan king, then called a meeting of the Peloponnesian League and urged them to restore Hippias, but the League members rebuffed him.

Sparta's intervention in Athens was only the first in a long line of attempts to dominate a captured city through the support of a pro-Spartan oligarchy, a method which seldom proved effective unless the oligarchs were able to develop a strong power base. Democratic states controlled by Sparta in this way invariably did not hold fast in their loyalty for any length of time.

With the end of the main phase of the war with Persia in 479 BC, Sparta turned inwards and spent the next twenty years consolidating her position in the Peloponnese. When in 460 BC she had finally quelled a long and troublesome helot revolt she emerged from her isolation and soon embroiled herself in an indecisive war with Athens which continued desultorily until 446 BC. The conflict did succeed, however, in reducing the size of Athens' land empire, which had reached its largest extent in 457 BC. After a brief lull, the Peloponnesian War erupted in 431 BC between the Peloponnesian League and the Athenian empire. Until this period Sparta had had few foreign possessions to regulate and her previous methods had proved successful.

Because of the state of war, however, the support of pro-Spartan oligarchs and enrolment in the Peloponnesian League no longer gave Sparta sufficient power over these conquered states. Consequently she began to station garrisons in some states, especially outside the Peloponnese. During the last decade of the war she was increasingly forced to garrison her conquests, primarily for military reasons but also to keep the populace in order. But it was not until she had emerged victorious that Sparta had to cope with the problem of incorporating and administering conquered cities on anything but a small scale.

After she had defeated Athens in 404 BC Sparta had her chance at empire, but she failed because she lacked efficient means of ruling and absorbing her conquests. Her treatment of Athens at the end of the Peloponnesian War provides a particular example of this weakness. Sparta spared Athens, probably because she did not wish to create a power vacuum in Attica into which she believed Thebes would move from the north. Her assessment of Thebes' intentions soon proved correct. Almost immediately after the end of the war, the Thebans initiated an anti-Spartan policy and tried to extend their influence into Attica. Thebes harboured Athenian exiles, whom she refused to yield to Sparta. Sparta tried to govern Athens through a board of thirty 'tyrants', chosen from among her adherents in the city. Because of internal dissension in Sparta, however, the moderate democrats had gained power in Athens within little more than a year and with this turn of events Sparta's domination of Athens was greatly weakened. By 395 BC Athens had joined Thebes to repel a Spartan invasion of Boeotia, which resulted in the Quadruple Alliance of Athens, Thebes, Argos and Corinth against Sparta. Having been compelled to dismantle her walls at the end of the Peloponnesian War, by 395/394 Athens was rapidly rebuilding her fortifications. The year 393 saw the completion of the walls, and Athens soon had the strength to stand once more against Sparta.

Sparta attempted to administer the empire which she had acquired through the war by the same methods which she had employed at Athens. In many cities the Spartan general Lysander established his minions: an oligarchic board of ten, called a 'decarchy', and a Spartan garrison under a 'harmost', a military officer, ruled and oppressed each city. These garrisons were supported by the tribute from the occupied cities. In Miletus, for example, Lysander had the democrats massacred and then set up a decarchy over what was left of the populace. These narrow boards created oligarchies in name, but tyrannies in fact. This repressive, rigid system of rule could not long endure without incurring revolts, and by 402 BC Lysander's influence was waning. At that time, alarmed at the complaints about the decarchies, Sparta either substituted broader oligarchies or allowed the cities to revert to their previous forms of government, probably with a concomitant reduction in the strength and numbers of garrisons. When King Agesilaus embarked on his campaign in Asia Minor in 396 BC, he reinstituted extreme oligarchies, though they were not as limited as Lysander's. After the Persians had defeated the Spartan fleet at Cnidos in 394 BC, almost all the states in the Aegean revolted – with the exception of the few which were adequately garrisoned – and at one stroke most of the Aegean empire which Sparta had acquired from Athens slipped from her grasp.

Nevertheless, Sparta continued to dominate subject states through oligarchies and garrisons. In 381 BC she ordered Phlius to receive back her exiled oligarchs and almost inevitably, as soon as the oligarchs returned, they set upon the democrats. The ensuing civil war gave Sparta the excuse she needed. She attacked and captured the town, garrisoned it, and imposed an oligarchic constitution, precisely what she had initially planned. In 382 Phoebidas, a Spartan officer, conspired with the oligarchic minority in Thebes and seized the citadel, the Cadmea. After the swift execution of the democratic leader and the flight of many democrats to Athens, Sparta sent troops to occupy the Cadmea, which was the dominant military position in the city. Sparta next installed pro-Spartan oligarchies in neighbouring Thespiae, Orchomenus and Plataea. Sometimes she destroyed cities as political entities in order to dominate the populace. In 386 she delivered an ultimatum to the Mantineans to raze their fortifications. They refused, and Sparta attacked. Defeated, the populace of Mantinea was divided into five separate villages, each of which had to furnish troops to Sparta.

By 379 BC, when her power had reached its greatest extent, Sparta permitted her allies, in lieu of military service, to substitute cash payments with which she hired mercenaries. In 378, however, the Thebans regained control of their city, and that marked the beginning of the rapid decline of Spartan power. Athens quickly joined with Thebes against Sparta and soon after founded the Second Athenian Confederacy. At the same time, Thebes, under the able leadership of Epaminondas and Pelopidas, was swiftly growing more powerful. The cities of Boeotia reconstituted their League, and this time, since they were willing to sacrifice some of their autonomy for the unified power of the League, they were able to form virtually a single state with Thebes as the centre of government.

In 371 the Thebans broke Spartan power at the battle of Leuctra and relegated her to the second rank from the position as the leading military state in Greece which she had held for two hundred years. The final blow came in 370 when Epaminondas freed the Messenian helots and created an independent state in Messenia. One reason for Sparta's defeat was her inability to adapt to changing military tactics. She had won her empire by the sword and when the sword rusted her empire dissolved. Her inability to deal successfully with her conquests and to forge them into some form of durable union was also a major reason for her decline. Unlike Athens, she had no common economic ties with her subjects and allies; her subjection of a state offered it few advantages, and her rigid conservatism hindered her from developing any innovatory means of coping with her conquests.

A drastic decrease in the citizen population contributed to Sparta's deterioration and failure after the Peloponnesian War. Continuous warfare in the fifth century had greatly diminished the citizen body, which bore the brunt of the fighting. As men were killed, there was no source of new blood to fill the ranks. A rapidly falling birth-rate further exacerbated the problem. Land problems, in part, were responsible for the decline in births. The ancient sources record that the *kleros* was inalienable. Plutarch notes that each citizen received a *kleros* at his birth (which probably reverted to the state at his death). Aristotle surmised that originally some type of alienable land had existed, and his conjecture seems likely to have been right, in view of the gross inequalities in land which existed but which would have been impossible if everyone had been restricted only to his assigned *kleros*. In the seventh century the *kleros* probably yielded enough produce to support the Spartiate and his helots and to allow him to contribute to the common table. As the wealth of Greece grew in the sixth and fifth centuries, however, the bare minimum produced by the *kleros* did not satisfy the increased desires and needs of the Spartans. At this time we hear of an ever-growing number of *hypomeiones* or 'inferiors', who are thought to be those who had lost full citizenship through failure to perform their obligations under the Lycurgan code. Thus private property became essential as a supplementary means of sustenance. But since every new-born citizen was entitled to a *kleros*, increases in population would require the creation of new *kleroi*. The state, therefore, would have to appropriate new allotments from alienable land held in private hands. The individual could no longer count on maintaining his personal holdings with security. The response of the citizenry was to preserve their recent prosperity by limiting the number of their children, a fact which may be deduced from laws designed to combat this trend, such as one which exempted a father of three sons from military duty.

Towards the end of the fifth century two classes of citizens, the *hypomeiones* and the emancipated helots (called *neodamodeis*, new citizens), became prominent. A shortage of manpower quickly made itself felt at the inception of the Peloponnesian War, before which military engagements had been of short duration and had been limited to conflicts between small city states. Even the war against Persia had been decided by a few major isolated battles. Now the Athenian empire was pitted against the Peloponnesian League and the fighting was costly and continuous. From the end of the main phase of the Persian War in 479 BC to the battle of Leuctra in 371 the number of Spartiates in the field steadily declined, from an estimated 5,000 in 479 BC to some 1,050 in 371. Sparta, a military state which had oppressed its helots for several centuries and had fought off a major revolt in the 460s, would not have armed, trained and freed those helots unless compelled to do so by extraordinary circumstances. In 424 BC helots were first used as soldiers when seven hundred of them accompanied Brasidas on his Thracian campaign. In recompense for service they were to obtain freedom and some citizenship rights. What rights they gained are uncertain, but they were not made 'equals'. The number of *neodamodeis* increased steadily, while the *hypomeiones* remained a small class. When Agesilaus went to Asia Minor in 396, two thousand *neodamodeis* accompanied him, who, when emancipated, would nearly outnumber Spartan citizens. Thus, after 424 BC, the Spartan army consisted of Spartiates (the so-called 'equals'), *perioikoi, neodamodeis* and a few *hypomeiones*. At the beginning of the fifth century, the *perioikoi* fought as a separate body in the army, as they probably did later in the century, and this arrangement was probably also applied to the other non-citizen contingents.

The ranks of the full citizens could only be swelled by new blood from what were called the *mothakes*, whose number was minuscule. It is uncertain exactly who the *mothakes* were, but they seem to have been men with only one 'equal' parent (Lysander himself was reputed to be one). They pursued the normal system of military training and could be made full Spartans, though this was uncommon. Dissatisfaction among the new classes grew continually, until at the beginning of the fourth century it culminated in an abortive revolt by the helots, *perioikoi* and other non-equals. Cinadon, the leader of the plot, and his followers were discovered, however, before the revolt began. They were bound fast, neck and arms, in collars, and were whipped and struck with goads as they were dragged through the city to their deaths. Within thirty years of this event, however, the helots were in possession of their own state.

In addition to these problems, the Spartan economy remained sluggish and static. Trade was almost non-existent, nor was there industrial production of goods. In the seventh, the sixth and even the fifth century the Spartan system had worked, but by the end of the fifth century it became fossilized and archaic, unable to adapt, no longer viable and ill-suited for empire. Unlike that of other nations, Sparta's military expansion did not produce a vigorous domestic economy nor increased wealth for the members of the state. Military domination and federation were the only means at her disposal for ruling her conquests and their success was limited from the outset. Her rigid social framework obviously precluded the expansion of her citizen body and of her influence as a unifying force in the Greek world.

ATHENIAN IMPERIALISM

Athens dealt with empire in a much more flexible and successful manner than Sparta. Her great period of empire began in the early fifth century in the aftermath of the war between Greece and Persia. The Persian War marked the beginning of the decline of the polis as an autonomous political unit. The polis functioned successfully as long as it was able to provide for its citizens in war and peace from its own resources. But with the advent of the Persian War Greece was faced with an enemy that no one city state could hope to combat. The city states were thus compelled to band together to meet this enemy, and once this had happened the polis could never again return to her isolation, even when the threat of an external enemy had been removed. After the war Athens transformed her allies into members of the Athenian empire. None of them was in a position to resist her supremacy. Any state that she threatened was forced either to join her or to adhere to the other major power bloc, the Peloponnesian League. This state of affairs was formalized by the terms of the Thirty Years' Peace in 446 BC, in which Athens and Sparta recognized each other's spheres of influence. No member was allowed to switch sides, while neutrals could join either bloc.

Through her empire Athens came closer to unifying Greece than any other state. Although she jealously guarded her own citizenship, she constantly fought against disruptive tendencies in her empire and did much to create a cohesive group of states. Athens was well aware of the importance of citizenship as a unifying element, as the institution of the cleruchy proves. Indeed, as we shall see at the end of this section, the evidence suggests that, had her empire endured longer, she might ultimately have bestowed citizenship upon its members.

When the Persians led their expedition against Greece in 481 BC the Greeks formed the Hellenic League, an offensive-defensive alliance under the leadership of Sparta. Although a Spartan general commanded the common forces, policy was formulated by all the states. After the defeat of the invader, however, internal problems, among other factors, caused Sparta to cede her role as chief state. As a maritime power with colonies in the Aegean, Athens was concerned with continuing the fight against Persia and protecting the Ionian cities and islands along the Asia Minor coast. Thus in 478/477 she and her Greek allies met at Delos, where a new entity, the Delian League, was formed for this purpose. The members signified that the League was permanent by casting a lead weight into the water and taking an oath to remain united until the weight should rise to the surface.

The Delian League was not simply an expanded version of the Hellenic League. The old League had mostly been composed of mainland states, and later a few islands, while the Delian League primarily comprised the Greek cities of the Aegean islands and coast, and was therefore based chiefly on naval rather than land power. The League's first purpose was to liberate the Greeks of the west coast of Asia Minor and thereafter to maintain their independence. Its members also craved Persian spoils from conquest and from raids on land and sea. Athens, as the most powerful member, was recognized as the leader. Although initially policy was decided by an equal vote of all members, Athens quickly became supreme; the lesser states sided with her because of her military might and influence. Athens took the command of all campaigns and the responsibility for raising and maintaining a fleet. Money and ships were needed to accomplish this, so the League established Delos as the site of its treasury and inaugurated a system of self-assessments of ships and money, with Athens acting as financial officer. Some states, however, were permitted to substitute monetary contributions for the ships or parts of ships they had been obligated to provide, and this arrangement allowed Athens to build a homogeneous navy of her own, instead of commanding heterogeneous flotillas; it thus increased the military dependence of the members, and undermined their position of equality in the League.

Gradually Athens exercised a greater voice in determining the assessments and exacted payment by force if necessary. Contribution was becoming tribute. The first threat to the unity of the League arose when the island of Naxos, dissatisfied with the League, attempted to secede in 470 BC. The League reacted swiftly to repair this damaging situation before it could spread. Naxos was decisively defeated, reduced in status, forbidden to keep a navy and forced to pay tribute instead of contributing ships. The historian Thucydides saw this as the beginning of the enslavement of the allied cities. Henceforth, loss of autonomy was meted out as punishment to rebel states who were either unwilling or unable to continue paying their assessments. Other revolts followed with increasing frequency. The island of Thasos quarrelled with Athens about mining rights in 465 and tried to withdraw from the League, but was subdued after a siege of two years. The Thasians were forced to dismantle their walls, surrender their ships, pay an immediate indemnity, and for the future to pay tribute to Athens. In the early years of the League no distinction was made between those who supplied ships and those who paid tribute; gradually, however, the latter came to be regarded as belonging to the same class as the subject allies (those who had lost autonomy). Their number multiplied steadily, until by 431 BC almost all the members of the League were *de facto* in this class.

Athens also forcibly enrolled any state she conquered as a subject ally in the League. In 457 she defeated the island of Aegina, a longtime trade rival. Aegina lost her navy, was forced to raze her fortifications, and was enrolled as a tribute ally. With Athens' victory over Thebes at Oenophyta in 457 all Boeotia with the exception of Thebes herself came under Athenian domination and was forced to join the League. In Boeotia Athens installed local democrats in power as a further means of controlling the region. These measures only partially succeeded and in 447 BC, to counteract the growing unrest, Athens sent Tolmides to Boeotia with one thousand hoplites. This was too small a force to restore Athenian supremacy, however, and the

55, 56 Two coins of Aegina, the hostile island state known to Athenians as 'the eyesore of the Piraeus'. Stripped of her maritime power by Athens in 457 BC, Aegina's coinage, hitherto distinguished by the symbol of a marine turtle (left), adopted that of the terrestrial tortoise.

expedition was a disaster; Tolmides and many of his men were killed, and a sufficiently large number of Athenians were captured to allow the Thebans to exact Athenian withdrawal from Boeotia as their ransom.

In 454/453 BC the treasury of the League was removed from Delos to Athens, thereby confirming openly what had in fact gradually occurred, the transformation of the Delian League into the Athenian empire. At this time Athens began to appropriate one-sixtieth of the tribute for the Goddess Athena; in 447/446 Pericles began with this money his famous building programmes at Athens for the glorification of his city.

A few years earlier, in 449/448, the Peace of Callias, concluded between Persia and the Delian League, formally brought an end to hostilities, and with it vanished much of the *raison d'être* for the existence of the League. Athens had no intention, however, of surrendering her hard-won position, and Pericles wasted little time in offering new justifications for the continuation of the existing arrangements. He appealed to the cause of Panhellenism, to the maintenance of freedom of the seas, and to the dictates of religious piety, which necessitated the restoration of the temples destroyed many years previously by the Persians.

In 440 BC two members of the League, Samos and Miletus, in a dispute over control of Priene, went to war. Miletus had revolted from Athens in the mid-450s; she had been conquered, made a tribute-paying ally, and had her navy disbanded. She revolted again in 446/445, at which time Athens established a democratic government. Samos, on the other hand, was an autonomous ally, with a very strong navy. Because of her naval superiority Samos quickly gained the upper hand, which drove Miletus to appeal to Athens for aid. Athens decided to intervene for two reasons. Firstly, she had obligations to Miletus as one of her subjects, especially since by removing her navy she had left her virtually defenceless. Secondly, to keep her empire strong and herself in control, Athens could not tolerate war between members of the League. The fact that Miletus was a democracy and Samos an oligarchy may have also influenced Athens.

Athens first asked the Samians to submit the dispute to arbitration. On their refusal Athens attacked. After an initial Athenian victory, a democracy was set up, but, as soon as the Athenian fleet withdrew, the Samian oligarchs regained control and turned to Persia for aid. Incited by the unrest in the empire, Byzantium now revolted and was followed by some cities in Caria, Thrace and Chalcidice; Mytilene too was on the point of revolt. The Samian oligarchs also appealed to the Peloponnesians for aid, but the latter refused to interfere, in observance of the terms of the Thirty Years' Peace. The revolts remained localized, and Athens swiftly subdued the other recalcitrant states and defeated Samos at her leisure, after a long siege in 439 BC. The Samians were treated leniently; they were compelled to raze their walls, dismantle their fleet and pay an indemnity, but no garrison or cleruchs were sent, nor tribute imposed on them at this time. Byzantium was brought into line with only minor penalties, as were the other cities. By the crushing of the Samian revolt and by her tolerant treatment of the rebels Athens had strengthened the empire, at least for the time being. Apart from Athens Samos was the strongest state in the League, and in bringing her to heel Athens had left no city in the League which could approach her in power. An example was set for the other cities: if the strongest of them could not successfully revolt, the rest surely had no hope of success.

By the outbreak of the Peloponnesian War in 431 BC only two allies, Chios and Lesbos, were still autonomous, and hostility to Athenian rule ran high in these cities. In 428 Mytilene, the most powerful city on Lesbos, joined by three smaller cities of the island, seceded from the League. She chose this moment because of Athens' temporary weakness. In 429 a devastating smallpox plague had struck Athens and

57 The Parthenon, most renowned of the temples of Greece and greatest of the new buildings begun in Athens under Pericles, buildings which 'seemed to have within them some everlasting breath of life' (Plutarch). ▶

killed great numbers, including Pericles, and the city was further shaken by continual Spartan invasions of Attica. Athens demanded Mytilene's surrender, and, confronted by defiance, besieged the city. The Mytileneans sent to Sparta with a request for admittance into the Peloponnesian League and begged for military assistance. Sparta hesitated, and by the time she dispatched ships the Mytileneans had almost been reduced to starvation. Although they knew Spartan help was on the way, the critical situation forced the oligarchs of Mytilene into immediate action. They armed the citizens for a strike against the Athenians. Once armed, however, the citizens turned on their oligarchs, who, in the face of internal dissension, had no recourse but to surrender to Athens. The assembly in Athens voted to execute every man in the city and to sell the women and children into slavery. A galley was sent from Athens to deliver the grim order, but the assembly, reconsidering their precipitous response, dispatched a second ship in the wake of the first with an order countermanding the execution. Rowing day and night, even eating at their oars, they arrived at their destination barely in time, and only the ringleaders at Mytilene were executed.

In 425 Athens reassessed and increased the tribute. This action provoked some discontent in the empire, particularly in the Thracian communities, where the energetic military activity of the Spartan general Brasidas in the 420s caused Scione and Mende, among others, to revolt. Amphipolis was betrayed by its citizens to Brasidas. After a long siege Athens retook Scione and this time imposed the full penalty for revolt, the execution of the male population and the enslavement of the women and children.

The unity Athens had temporarily imposed on her subject city states proved fragile at best. It was continually threatened by the resentment of her subjects, who objected to the high cost imposed upon the members of the League, both in the financial drain on their resources and in the erosion of their traditional autonomy. At the opening of the Peloponnesian War Sparta was able to advance as one justification for abrogating her treaty with Athens the plight of the tribute cities, to whom she offered the promise of liberation and a restoration of independence.

The Peace of Nicias brought a temporary halt to the Peloponnesian War in 421 BC. By its terms the cities in the north-west Aegean that had revolted from Athens were guaranteed their autonomy, so long as they paid tribute, but could rejoin the alliance if they wished.

Problems with her allies diminished, until Athens came into conflict with Melos in 416 BC. This small island was a non-belligerent ally of Sparta, with an excellent location and harbour. Consequently Athens had attempted to coerce her into joining the empire as early as 426, in which year Athens had staged an unsuccessful raid against her. Despite this failure Athens included Melos in the tribute lists of 425/424 BC; but Melos naturally refused to pay. After a long lull, in 416 an Athenian expedition was dispatched to conquer the island. Upon their victory at the end of a costly and exasperating siege the Athenians, desirous of making an example, executed every man on Melos still left alive and sold every woman and child into slavery. This act was a usual punishment for colonies which had revolted, but severe in a case of original conquest such as this. Athens then settled cleruchs on the island.

Not until two Athenian armies had been annihilated at Syracuse in 413 BC and the defeat of Athens loomed imminently did Athens' allies begin to desert her. Euboea, Lesbos, Erythrae and Chios sent embassies to Sparta. Sparta first accepted the Chians and then the Erythraeans as allies. The loss of Chios was a particularly hard blow to Athens. After Corcyra and Athens she was the strongest naval power in the empire and brought sixty ships with her to the Peloponnesian side. Clazomenae followed Chios' lead, as did Miletus. The Chians then induced Lebedos and Haerae to revolt, while Sparta persuaded the inhabitants of Methymna and Mytilene to do likewise. Some of these cities, however, were gradually regained by Athens.

The Athenian empire depended on sea power for its existence and its strength. As Chios and Sparta encroached on her absolute control of the sea, it became increasingly difficult for Athens to hold her empire together, and her growing weakness offered her subject states the opportunity to revolt with minimal risk. The fact that many did not suggests the strong allegiance they felt towards Athens. The failure of a city to revolt, however, does not necessarily imply loyalty, since many other motives, such as fear of reprisal or economic dependence, might be involved. Thucydides viewed the Athenian empire as a selfish despotism, hated by its oppressed and exploited subjects. Had this one-sided view been the case, however, we would have expected cities to revolt, at least where and when it was feasible. When, on the contrary, a city chose not to revolt in the face of extreme pressure and the threat of certain annihilation by the Spartans, we may deduce her favourable disposition towards Athens.

During Brasidas' Thracian campaigns most towns surrendered, but some withstood his onslaught, despite his superior force. Brasidas took Torone through betrayal, but some of its citizens attacked the Scionian and Peloponnesian garrison. In Acanthus, Sane, Dium and Torone, most citizens displayed loyalty to Athens. The Chian defection from Athens in 412 BC was apparently caused by a combination of expediency and oligarchic plots. The oligarchic faction in the city plotted to establish an oligarchy and then to revolt from the Athenian empire. Because of the weakness of their position and public hostility to oligarchy, however, they delayed any action until the arrival of Spartan troops, accompanied by Alcibiades (who at that juncture was fighting for Sparta). The Spartan troops in concert with the oligarchs, after executing the leaders of the pro-Athenian democratic leaders, set up an oligarchy. However, the oligarchs failed to win the loyalty of the populace, and certain Chians plotted to betray the city to the Athenians when they later besieged it.

In 412/411 BC the Spartan commander Astyochus attacked Athenian allies on the mainland opposite Chios, but failed to take even the small town of Pteleum, which refused to surrender. Thasos, where Athens had tolerated an oligarchy, did not revolt, but pursued a more or less autonomous neutrality until 407 BC, when Thrasybulus brought her back into the empire by force. Her neighbour Neapolis remained loyal, for which the Athenians voted her special privileges. On the island of Lesbos, the cities of Methymna and Mytilene defected to Sparta in 412, but were soon recovered; thereafter Mytilene remained faithful even after the final Athenian defeat at Aegospotami. Other cities stood fast. Cedreae in Caria stoutly resisted Lysander in 405, and as her punishment was plundered and her inhabitants enslaved. Lampsacus opposed Lysander and was plundered. Carian Iasus was sacked by the Spartans in 412 for not yielding. Yet despite this first lesson she remained loyal to Athens and in 405 resisted Lysander so fiercely that when at length he took the city by storm, he executed the males and enslaved the remainder of the population.

When the Syracusans defeated the Athenian army in Sicily in 413 BC, they offered freedom to any of the islanders among the Athenian forces who would desert to them. Resistance was obviously hopeless and death imminent, but few went over to the enemy. Plato remarked that Athens kept her rule for seventy years because she had friends in every city. The defections during the Thracian campaign of the 420s and the Ionian campaign of 412–404 are not a fair test of Athenian popularity, because of the military pressures which induced revolts. On the whole, in fact, the loyalty shown to Athens by her allies was remarkable, both by states under extreme military pressure and by those in normal circumstances.

Athens controlled her empire by many means, the most important of which were military and economic, although she also successfully employed constitutional and legal avenues. Thus, Athens regulated commercial litigation in the empire. Between Athens and her allies various trade treaties existed, such as the Phaselis decree, which, among other things, provided that any lawsuit arising over trade between Athenians and Phaselites would be heard at Athens. Trade treaties varied in significance according to the status of the ally. In the case of independent allies, they contained provisions relating to the judgment of civil cases concerning members of subject states. With Miletus, for example, civil suits over a certain sum were transferred to Athens. Many civil cases, particularly those involving litigation between allied states or their citizens, were heard at Athens, as were serious criminal offences. Athens became the appeal court in all cases involving the death penalty. Gradually Athens became the legal centre of the empire.

Athens encouraged democratic forms of government throughout the empire, because democracies tended to be more loyal to her. But she did not ruthlessly overthrow oligarchies, Aristotle notwithstanding. When a state revolted Athens naturally sided with the democratic faction and set up a democracy once the revolt had been crushed. This happened in Erythrae, Colophon, Chalcis and Samos among others. But oligarchies were tolerated in a few cities. In Miletus after the revolt of 450/449 an oligarchy was allowed. Athens did not interfere with the oligarchy at Potidaea, so long as that state remained a loyal member of the empire. The prevalence of democracies in the empire was partially caused by the fact that trading states, which comprised most of the empire, tended to produce commercial classes who favoured democracy, while agricultural states tended towards oligarchy.

It should not be supposed that democracy was everywhere the most popular form of government. In many places the leading families had considerable followings – sometimes including a majority of the population – who preferred to be governed by their traditional rulers rather than by their own equals. Consequently, when Athens overthrew the oligarchy in such a state and installed a 'democracy', the new 'democrats' were well aware that their power – and, often, even their lives – were safe only so long as they supported Athens and Athens them. This accounts for the faithfulness of many 'democratic' governments to Athens, even in the face of certain defeat. Such cases have been pointed out already. Samos is a good example. The Samian 'democrats' had kept themselves in power through the last half of the Peloponnesian War by murdering all the oligarchs they could find; they knew what was in store for them if Athens fell and thus they remained 'loyal' to Athens even after she had fallen. Another factor was financial. Athens had a big naval base at Samos which must have given employment to a large proportion of the island's population.

Athens also sent out administrative officials throughout the empire. According to Aristotle there were seven hundred Athenian officials in the empire in the fifth century, or an average of two to three officials per city. These officials were called *archontes*. Their number varied with the size and importance of the city to which they were attached, and the extent of Athenian control. There were five *archontes* in Colophon in 447 BC, while on the small unimportant island of Sciathus in 408/407 there was only one. If the city was garrisoned, the garrison commander was one of the *archontes*. Most of the *archontes* were inspectors (*episkopoi*). The Erythrae decree of about 452 BC mentions the presence of inspectors and garrison commanders. The inspectors were to establish a new Erythraean council. Although they interfered with the local governments in civil matters, the main function of inspectors was to supervise Athenian interests, particularly by enforcing Athenian decrees and by assisting in the collection of tribute. In those states where they settled, cleruchs, as Athenian citizens, naturally aided the *archontes* in supporting Athens.

Athenian garrisons were also maintained in many states in the empire. Their chief function was to ensure Athenian military superiority in the regions where they were stationed. Secondarily they provided some measure of control for Athens over her allies, though the need to use military forces in this respect was generally minimal. Athens began garrisoning on a large scale in the 450s, primarily to strengthen her military power in the face of Sparta's growing might, rather than as a means of controlling her colonies. Aegina and Erythrae had garrisons from an early time, as did Miletus. By 440 BC Colophon, Chalcis, Halicarnassus and Mytilene, among many other cities, were garrisoned. Such cities were required to pay for the garrisons quartered on their soil. Despite their strategic military purpose, however, the garrisons infringed on the sovereignty of the states where they were stationed.

In conjunction with the inspectors, they exercised military and some political control over the city, and provided the potential force to ensure the maintenance of Athenian interests.

Athenian control over her empire was wielded in the main through economic leverage. Most of the states in the empire were maritime, either islands or coastal cities. As such, their commerce depended on the sea. Either they were traders themselves or they needed or desired to import goods which they did not produce, particularly wheat. Xenophon makes clear the commercial importance of Athens: 'and every traveller who would cross from one to the other end of Greece', he writes, 'passes Athens as the centre of a circle . . . she possesses the finest and safest accommodation for shipping. . . . At most other ports merchants are compelled to ship a return cargo, because their local currency has no circulation in other states, but at Athens they have the opportunity of exchanging their cargo and exporting very many classes of goods that are in demand, or if they do not want to ship a return cargo of goods, they can export silver.'

Because of her silver-mines and the tribute from her allies, Athens had much money at her disposal. She imported many products, particularly grain. She became the main market in the empire for a variety of goods, such as raisins, figs, spices, flax, wool, furniture and carpets. We have already noted Pericles' remarks on the range of Athenian imports. At the same time Athens exported olive oil, wine, marble and pottery. For many cities Athens was a wealthy customer with which to deal and she also kept the seas safe for commerce. Thus the members of the empire derived economic benefits in exchange for their tribute. The economic strength of Athens was reflected by the Megarian decree, whereby Athens excluded Megara, a prominent member of the Peloponnesian League, from the ports of the empire and the Piraeus, the port of Athens. This was such an economically crushing blow for Megara that it became a *casus belli* for the Peloponnesian War.

Besides the natural economic domination that Athens exercised over her empire, she made attempts to set up other economic controls. Most important of these was the standardization of money. At first she did not interfere much with island coinage, but as Athens gained firmer control one island after another ceased to mint coins. Paros and Siphnos minted coins until about 450, after which year they appear on the tribute lists and no longer struck coins until the end of the fifth century. Independent coinage probably ceased in Aegina in 456 when

93

58 Late sixth-century vase-painting of two warships under sail. Built up by far-sighted statesmen such as Themistocles, Athenian sea power was to become the indispensable foundation of her imperial hegemony.

she became part of the empire. From 445, when she was conquered by Pericles, until 411, when she regained her independence, Euboea did not mint coins. In about 449 BC Athens passed a decree to regulate currency, forbidding both the minting of silver coins in cities in the empire and the use of non-Athenian currency, weights and measures. Though mints were closed in many cities, however, the ban on other coinage was not absolute, and Athens was unable to bring about the exclusive use of her coinage, particularly on the fringes of the empire – as is illustrated by the tribute lists of 429/428 BC, which contain entries in Aeginetan staters, Chian didrachms, Acanthian silver and 'mixed foreign silver'.

Athens dominated coinage in her colonies, the Aegean islands and cities of Asia Minor. Where she was unable to impose Attic currency, or chose not to, she usually forced at least the use of the Attic standard of weights, as in Samos and Rhodes. At the beginning of the fifth century the Aeginetan coinage was most widely used, but as Athens became more powerful the Aeginetan standard declined. The main rivals to Attic coinage were the Persian and Chian. The Chian coinage was influenced by the Aeginetan, which was used in the Peloponnese. After 412 BC, when Peloponnesian power grew in Asia Minor, the Chian coinage, easily convertible to the Aeginetan, became more widespread and its use vastly accelerated after the fall of Athens in 404.

Athens, in many respects, created a cohesive empire. Its basis was Athenian dominance as a sea power and an economic power. Athens was aware of the importance of unity and loyalty, and on the whole returned adequate services for the tribute which she collected. Through her use of cleruchs she learned the importance of citizenship as a means of binding a state to her, but with one exception she never admitted members of her empire to citizenship. Nevertheless it is possible that, had her empire survived the Peloponnesian War, she would have granted citizenship more widely. In his play *Lysistrata*, which was presented in 411 BC, Aristophanes makes a plea for everyone to be incorporated into the state, even metics and foreigners. Lysistrata suggests that the state be managed like fleece:

> *First in the washing-tub plunge it, and scour it,*
> *   and cleanse it from grease,*
> *Purging away all the filth and the nastiness. . . .*
> *Then you should card it, and comb it, and mingle it*
> *   all in one basket of love and of unity,*
> *Citizens, visitors, strangers, and sojourners,*
> *   all the entire, undivided community.*
> *Know you a fellow in debt to the Treasury?*
> *   Mingle him merrily in with the rest.*
> *Also remember the cities, our colonies,*
> *   outlying states in the east and the west,*
> *Scattered about to a distance surrounding us,*
> *   these are our shreds and our fragments of wool;*
> *These to one mighty political aggregate*
> *   tenderly, carefully, gather and pull,*
> *Twining them all in one thread of good fellowship;*
> *   thence a magnificent bobbin to spin,*
> *Weaving a garment of comfort and dignity,*
> *   worthily wrapping the people therein.*
>
> (tr. B. B. Rogers)

In fact, the only state which Athens ever admitted to full citizenship rights was Samos, and this occurred in an exceptional situation, at the

59 Mid-fifth-century coin of Samos. This coin type remained constant (with the addition of successive letters of the alphabet to indicate the sequence of issue) until 439 BC, when Athens conquered Samos and prohibited her from minting further coinage.

end of the Peloponnesian War, when Athens was already lost. The Athenian fleet had just been decisively defeated at the battle of Aegospotami in 405 BC and the fall of the city loomed ahead. After a democratic revolt, Samos sent word to Athens that she would fight with her until the end. In thanks, Athens bestowed full citizenship on the Samians – a gratuitous gesture, but one which would have been unthinkable a hundred years before, no matter what the circumstances.

GREEK IMPERIALISM IN RETROSPECT

Greek city states never developed successful means of integrating their conquests or joining together to form a united state. Possible exceptions to this were some of the later Hellenistic leagues, of which the individuals of each state were citizens. But by then it was too late for any general unity to develop or its effects to be influential, for foreign conquerors already dominated the country.

Although in very early periods citizenship might be given to a broad geographical area, such as Attica, states quickly solidified their territories and populations, and citizenship came to be a very closely guarded privilege. Democracies permitted more people to be citizens than did oligarchies, but both were very restrictive. Citizenship brought with it the privilege of ruling the state. Thus to grant citizenship to other states meant a sacrifice of autonomy. The pride in the city state and the individualism of the fifth century made this prospect anathema.

Greek city states lacked the innate desire to create a large cohesive state and their citizenship practices made it nearly impossible for them to absorb another state without changing their own basic structure. Consequently when one Greek city state conquered another domination, not integration, generally resulted. This was a two-edged sword; the conqueror could preserve his autonomy, but he was unable to gain firm and lasting control over the conquered.

In contrast, by the end of the Peloponnesian War, the polis no longer seemed politically viable. Its territory perhaps ravaged by war, its resources wasted, its population reduced in battle with the foe, and its spirit demoralized by internal dissensions and fluctuating standards, the state's ability to ensure collective survival could no longer command its citizens' confidence. The concept of the polis as a self-sufficient and self-limiting political entity, as a monolithic entity in itself, had always militated against political unity on a large and permanent scale. In late fifth- and early fourth-century Athens the political, social and spiritual crisis of the community encouraged poets, philosophers and statesmen to search for ways to renew the relationship of the individual and his society, and some turned to the ideal of Panhellenism as a saving force.

60 Warriors going off to battle; the frequent wars in which many Greek states were involved naturally dictated much of the social and political organization of the polis.

V INTERNAL PROBLEMS:
CLASS CONFLICT AND CIVIL WAR

Internal discord and civil war dogged the Greek city state throughout its history. With the breakdown of a static agrarian society in the eighth and seventh centuries, the non-aristocratic classes increasingly demanded and obtained full voting and office-holding rights. In the seventh and sixth centuries the Greek tyrant emerged, often as the champion of the new rich and the hoplites, and as an opponent of the old aristocrats. Economic changes in society, coupled with the force and energy of the Greek tyrants, served to break down the power of the old aristocracy. Once the tyrants had fulfilled their purpose of aiding the hoplites and the new moneyed class to win their rights, they were soon ousted. Left in their place were democracy and oligarchy. The fifth century was a period of great internal discord and civil war between oligarchs and democrats within the Greek states. The twenty-seven-year-long Peloponnesian War between Athens and Sparta in some ways became an ideological clash between these two forms of rule, Athens being the democracy and supporter of democrats, Sparta the oligarchy and supporter of oligarchs.

The history of the internal conflict and civil wars in Athens and in Greece is the history of the struggles of the lower classes to obtain from the upper classes equal citizenship rights and a full share in the rule of the state. For a clearer understanding of these struggles over citizenship, it is necessary first to examine the class structure of Greece.

THE GREEK SOCIAL SYSTEM
Because of the scantiness of sources and archaeological information, we can form only an approximate picture of Greek society. The society of the Dark Ages and archaic period was agrarian with a basic division between nobles and non-nobles. The subdivisions of these two groups were not sharply drawn and often overlapped. The nobles were divided into a loose hierarchy, at the top of which was the royal clan from which the king was drawn; probably the next most powerful group

was the priests, if indeed they comprised a separate class; and finally the rich landowners. The nobles may originally have been conquerors or simply wealthy landowners who, in the course of time, had become 'noble' through their position in society. Their nobility, based on force of arms or wealth, eventually became a nobility of birth and they came to be called 'the good', 'the blessed', 'the happy' and 'sons of noble fathers'. The non-noble portion of society was composed of three major segments. First were the peasant owners of medium- and small-sized land-holdings, called by the aristocrats 'the evil', 'the base' and 'the many'. Next came the *thetes*, free men who were not landholders but traders, craftsmen, and agricultural labourers. Finally there were the slaves.

The king, usually the head of the strongest aristocratic clan, was a tribal chieftain whose royal power was based on land and cattle. The community provided him with a *temenos*, or estate, and certain revenues. In the early periods wars were not fought to extend territory, but for booty, of which the king received the largest share. He could also call upon the labour of the citizens in times of need, for building ships or defence works. 'Gifts' were also given to the king by the people, but under compulsion. In the *Odyssey* King Alcinous, having decided to present gifts to Odysseus says to his nobles 'let us each give him a great tripod and cauldron; and we in turn shall gather among the people and be recompensed'. 'Gifts' lacked the regularity of taxes and were not usually as onerous. In return the king furnished protection and defence, and at times dispensed justice.

Although in some states, such as Corinth, the royal clan maintained control of the state as late as the seventh century, in general the kings soon lost their privileges and merged with the nobles, the royal clan deteriorating to the level of other aristocratic families. The king's position was based on religious, military and political leadership. In curtailing this power the aristocrats first usurped the military role and put one of their members in charge of military affairs as war-lord. Once they dominated the military organization, the aristocrats also rapidly won political control. The king, however, retained his religious duties and the guardianship of property rights, which were subsequently assumed first by members of the royal clan, then by the nobility in general, and finally by the state. This line of development can be seen in the workings of the government in the seventh and early sixth centuries in Athens. The state was administered by three officials called 'archons' ('rulers'), drawn from the ranks of the aristocracy.

The 'king' archon was invested with the responsibility for religious affairs, the archon who was 'general' commanded the military, and a third archon had political control.

Most of the wealth of the state, which was in the form of land and cattle, was in the hands of the aristocrats. The names of the clans and classes reflect this, for example the *geomoroi* or 'landholders'. The power of the aristocrats had been acquired through military superiority and this remained its basis. The nobles alone could afford the expensive armour and horses needed for warfare. In the Dark Ages and the archaic period a battle consisted of clashes between individual warriors, for organized infantry had not yet developed. In early Athenian noble ('Eupatrid') tombs corpses were buried with their swords; but with the curtailment of aristocratic power and the rise of the hoplite, weapons disappear from the graves of nobles. Society depended on the aristocrats for defence and protection, and the populace lacked the military capacity to seize power, even had it wished to do so. The military might of the nobles allowed them to dominate the political machinery and the tribe, which was the basic organizational unit of the polis. The control of the tribe was particularly important, since in the absence of public law it safeguarded the rights of its members, especially in cases of murder or inheritance.

The great dividing line between nobles and non-nobles was rarely crossed. Fundamentally the nobles and landowners differed only in the extent of their land and the size of their households, which consisted of family, retainers, *thetes* and slaves. But the economic structure

61 Individual combat in the Homeric manner: Achilles deals Hector his death blow beneath the walls of Troy.

of archaic society was such that there was simply no way for the medium-sized landowner to acquire more land. Increasing population, as we have seen, caused land to be further subdivided between heirs, who therefore became less willing to part with their land even if this had been possible. Since the economy was not a moneyed one, it became almost impossible to accumulate wealth and with it surmount the class barrier. Nor could a non-noble hope to bridge the class lines by marriage to a noble, since intermarriage was rare and socially unacceptable.

Most of the free population were peasants with their own holdings. Some belonged to a group called *demiourgoi* or 'those who work for the people'. They were tradesmen, carpenters and metalworkers, but refrained from agricultural employment. Their services were probably open for hire to the whole community.

The lowest class among the free men who worked for hire were, as has been noted, called *thetes*. Unlike the *demiourgos*, the *thes* was not a craftsman. In some ways his position was even lower than a slave's. Slaves were at least part of a household and had some form of identity, while *thetes* remained outside any social structure. It was the *thes*, not the slave, whom Achilles in the *Odyssey* saw as the lowest person in society when, visited in Hades by Odysseus, he lamented 'I would rather be bound down, working as a *thes* for another, by the side of a landless man whose livelihood was not great, than be a ruler of all the dead who have perished.'

Slavery, in fact, was not very extensive in the Dark Ages and archaic period. The few male slaves worked in houses, fields and vineyards. In contrast to later practice, they were not hired out. Because of the paucity of males and the considerable economic burden involved in raising their offspring, owners seldom mated their slaves. The economy did not require agricultural slaves. Generally when a city was captured the males were executed and the females and children made domestic slaves. Before the sack of Troy Hector in the *Iliad* expresses his forebodings to his wife Andromache: 'I care not so much for the grief of the Trojans hereafter ... as for yours, when one of the bronze-clad Achaeans will carry you off in tears, and you will be in Argos, working the loom at another woman's bidding, and you will draw water from Messeis or Hypereia.' Slave women worked in the household, washing, sewing, cleaning and grinding meal. If one were young and pretty she might be called upon to share the master's bed. This practice is implied in the *Odyssey* when it is said of the slave Eurycleia,

Odysseus' nurse, 'Laertes brought her . . . when she was still in the prime of youth . . . but he never had intercourse with her.'

In the archaic period, then, little opportunity for social or economic mobility existed. By the sixth and fifth centuries, however, the situation had considerably changed. Greek society continued to be segregated along similar general class lines, but in a less rigid and less unalterable fashion. An example is the Athenian woodsman, Timomachus, who lived in the country; he had a son who came to the city and became a woodworker; and his son, Timomachus' grandson, rose to the rank of general.

Class divisions now became based primarily on wealth; this was particularly true of the aristocratic pedigree, the hereditary basis of which began somewhat to diminish. The number of aristocrats had greatly decreased in proportion to the rest of the population, while the moderate and small landholders had grown in numbers and power, as had the landless citizens. The *thetes*, in particular, became engaged in the many diverse occupations found in urban centres. But the greatest change between the archaic and classical periods was the vast growth in the numbers of non–citizens, who might account for as much as 40 per cent of the population in such states as fifth-century Athens. The slave and freedman population had greatly increased and a new non–citizen commercial class of foreign businessmen had sprung up.

In classical society there existed a sharp demarcation between citizens and non-citizens. Citizens, however, were divided into classes which frequently overlapped, and the distinction between aristocrat and non-aristocrat became blurred. The aristocracy of the fifth century was a combination of the old one of birth and the new one of wealth. These aristocrats still had holdings primarily in land, but they might make capital investments in other areas of the economy or have other sources of income. The old nobility tried to maintain its identity – for example, nobles felt it to be their duty to compel heiresses to marry kinsmen in order to preserve the family estates. But they were gradually absorbed into the new aristocracy of wealth, and by the fourth century the only real aristocracy was one based almost exclusively on wealth.

Although the aristocrats had land-holdings, they tended, in this period, to move from their estates to the city, where they often found it convenient to become *rentiers*, men without profession who lived on the income from their estates and disdained work. In Thebes, for instance, shopkeepers were excluded from political office, but an individual shopkeeper would regain this right after ten years of retirement. In Sparta the Spartiate was forbidden by law to have a profession, even that of an artisan. Plato had only contempt for sophists who taught for money, and distinguished Socrates from them because he did not. Socrates urged a certain Eutherus, who had fallen on hard times, to take a post as a steward, but the latter's pride would not allow him to follow this occupation. As late as the first century AD Plutarch remarks that no gifted young man would want to be even a Pheidias or a Polycleitus, great sculptors of the past, since they were mere craftsmen, in the same class as perfumers and dyers.

The aristocrats no longer completely dominated religious life, though they still monopolized some important priesthoods; they lost control of the military resources of the state, however, entirely. New

THE LOWER CLASSES

62–66 Slaves, *thetes* and women provided the infrastructure on which classical Greek society depended. Below, slaves carrying pottery and selling

bread. Above, women carding and spinning wool in the home and (below) baking bread: private houses often functioned as small manufacturing workshops. Below right, comic actor portraying a street vendor.

types of warfare and armour and the emergence of sea power reduced their military role to insignificance.

The farms, even of the rich, were small by modern standards. In the sixth century Solon divided the citizens of Athens into classes according to wealth. A member of the highest class in his classification had to have an income of five-hundred *medimnoi* (roughly, bushels) of corn or its equivalent in other produce or money. To produce this amount one would need a minimum of about fifty to seventy-five acres of mixed cornfields and vineyards.

In Athens a majority of the citizens lived on or from the land as medium- and small-sized landholders. In the seventh and sixth centuries most lived in the country, and even at the end of the fifth century the farmers were not accustomed to the city and its ways. When repeated Spartan invasions of Attica during the Peloponnesian War forced them inside the city walls, they found city life extremely unfamiliar and difficult.

The landowners with medium-sized holdings, together with the more prosperous of the small farmers, served as hoplites in the military organization. Their political allegiance varied; often they supported a moderate democracy, but at times oligarchy. The smaller farmers, who tended to serve in the army as light-armed troops, generally allied themselves with the *thetes* and the more radical democrats.

While in the archaic age the *thetes* may have formed a relatively small part of the population, in the classical period they formed the

67–69 Every Greek city numbered a diversity of small craftsmen among its inhabitants. Either metics, slaves or *thetes*, they often became relatively

largest single class of citizens. In fifth-century Athens half of the citizen population were *thetes*. Some of them were very small farmers on tiny lots of land, which barely provided subsistence: some of these minuscule lots might have fetched as little as fifty drachmas. Most *thetes* sold their labour as fullers, cobblers, carpenters, smiths, retailers or peddlers. The more successful in these occupations accumulated enough money to rise in class. Some *thetes* hired themselves out as farm labourers. The surviving accounts for the building of the Erechtheum (409/408 BC) show that out of seventy contractors and workers, fifteen were citizens, most likely *thetes*.

In most Greek cities the development of trade and commerce stimulated the development of a new commercial class of foreign non-citizens, called 'metics'. At the same time the proportion of slaves increased astronomically in comparison to archaic times, since in the classical period, with the growth of industry, trade and mining, many new uses had been found for them. Metics, slaves and freedmen took little part in the internal class struggles in Greece, though individuals might join in the conflict between the democratic and oligarchic factions. In Corcyra at one point certain slaves aided the democratic faction against the oligarchs in exchange for a promise of their freedom.

The metic was a foreigner who had come to a city such as Athens to better his lot. In Athens foreigners were classified as temporary or permanent residents. The great majority were more or less permanent,

prosperous. Left, a fishmonger's shop, (centre) a vase-painter at work in a potter's workshop and (right) a cobbler measures a boy for a pair of shoes.

and usually the whole class was referred to by their name, metics or 'fellow dwellers'. The proportion of metics in Athens was higher than in most states, about 10 per cent of the population. They came from every geological location. Inscriptions of the fifth and fourth centuries refer to Thracians, Phrygians, Carians, Paphlagonians, Celts, Lydians, Syrians, Phoenicians, Egyptians, Arabs, Scythians and Persians. The metic was treated much like a citizen. He registered with the deme where he lived. In addition to paying the same taxes as a citizen, he was required to pay a nominal residential tax. According to his wealth, he had to serve in the army as a hoplite or in the fleet as a rower or sailor.

No limitations were placed on where he lived or what religion he practised. In fact, the Athenians were very much influenced by foreign religions. At the end of the fifth century Thracian, Phrygian, Syrian and Egyptian cults appeared and gained some popularity in Athens. The opening scene of Plato's *Republic*, for example, depicts Socrates on his return from observing the rites of the Thracian goddess Bendis which had just been introduced into the Piraeus at that time.

Metics greatly influenced the economic structure of the state since they came to dominate the crafts, trade and commerce, both foreign and domestic. Maritime commerce, which they controlled, did not yield much profit to the individual trader, and was largely conducted by separate voyages in small ships undertaken by financially insecure merchants on borrowed money. Those with capital might invest in these enterprises, but they took little direct part themselves. The very high rates of interest on bottomry loans suggest that foreign trade yielded substantial returns, but even if the voyage was successfully completed the trader's profit margin would have been reduced after the loans were repaid, and the voyage could easily fail. Most merchants were eager to abandon the business as soon as they had acquired some capital. In a speech by Demosthenes a trader states: 'For a long time I was a merchant and risked my own life at sea; but some seven years ago I left the sea to use my modest earnings in the bottomry business.' Although shipping was conducted by individual metics at great personal risk and large shipping concerns were seldom formed, the total amount of trading was considerable. Shipbuilding, too, came to be run by metics. It was not a large-scale industry, however, especially since a ship might ply her trade for as long as thirty or forty years with her small cargoes, if she did not sink first.

Metics produced most manufactured goods. Like trade, manufacturing was ordinarily conducted on a very small scale and individual workshops probably averaged no more than ten to fifteen workmen, usually slaves. The largest factory in Athens, the shield factory of Cephalus, was considered enormous with a work force of 120 slaves. The pottery trade from early days was dominated by metics, and craftsmen were generally non-citizens. Of the names of pottery-painters of the sixth and fifth centuries which are known, many are servile or foreign, such as 'The Lydian', Amasis and Syricus.

The metics as a class never pressed for citizenship, though certain individuals sought it quite actively. Citizenship was not of primary importance to most metics. Classes agitated for citizenship rights and exercised those rights only when they would bring advantage, either in material terms or in increased freedom and status; and this was normally not the case for metics. Their position outside the citizen framework allowed the metics much social mobility. One would expect to find a rich metic like Cephalus in the home of an aristocrat, but be surprised to meet a citizen *zeugites* there. The metics had both the advantages and the obligations of citizens. They could, it is true, own no real property; as non-citizens they were forbidden to hold public office, and were not allowed to appear in court on their own behalf; they were also excluded from some occupations connected with land, such as mining. They did, however, hold all the other civil and property rights of citizens; their life was generally stable and their businesses profitable. They tended to be uninterested in holding public office and suffered little from their exclusion from it. Only if the metics had lost their position of relative security, and had needed political power to maintain their rights and privileges, might they have agitated for political power.

The most important factor which prevented metics from entering into the class struggle and pressing for citizenship, however, was psychological. The idea that citizenship is a right rather than a privilege is a relatively modern one. Today citizenship is usually acquired by virtue of one's birth in a state. There are few, if any, ethnic, racial or tribal prerequisites. In ancient Greece the city state was basically an outgrowth of the tribal structures. Membership in the state also entailed belonging to a tribe. Partially as a result of this situation, great particularism existed in the Greek polis. Both the foreigner in Athens and the Athenian would view the foreigner as a member of his original city. Neither would consider it the right of the foreigner to be given citizenship in Athens merely because he had settled there or was born there. He might be granted the privileges of citizenship, but only if he performed some great deed for the state. The case of Lysias is typical. His father, a wealthy Syracusan named Cephalus (his house was the setting for Plato's *Republic*), had settled in Athens at the invitation of Pericles. Lysias was born in Athens. He supplied money, weapons and his own services to the democratic revolt against the infamous Thirty Tyrants in 404/403 BC. After the defeat of the Tyrants, the Athenians, flushed with gratitude, awarded many metics, including Lysias, citizenship for their assistance. As soon as conditions settled, however, the requirements for the granting of citizenship were stiffened, and Lysias and many of the other metics who had won their citizenship were returned to their former status. Given this attitude on the part of the state and of the metics themselves, we can see why they never pressed for citizenship. Since their own rights were not at stake in the oligarchic-democratic struggles over who should rule, the metics seldom became involved unless they themselves or their property came under direct attack.

For many of the same reasons as the metics, freedmen and slaves likewise did not participate in the class struggles within the Greek states nor agitate for freedom and citizenship. Slavery derived from three sources: birth, judicial condemnation and war. Very few were born in the house. Breeding was not profitable, mainly because of the high infant mortality rate. Except in the early sixth century, insolvent debtors in Athens were not enslaved. Thus war was the major source of slaves, and the great marts of Byzantium, Ephesus, Chios and Thessaly flourished. Most slaves, whether taken in war or purchased, were non-Greek; they included Sarmatians, Persians, Arabs, Egyptians, Libyans and Thracians.

Although slaves made up about 25 per cent of the population of Athens, Athenian society was not dependent on them for its economic existence, nor was the democratic system built upon slavery. Except for domestics and those working in the mines, slaves were not strictly essential for the citizens' well-being. Unlike those in Rome in the second century BC, or in the southern states of the United States in the nineteenth century, in Greece slaves were of little value in agriculture because the land was simply too poor. Most agriculture was conducted on a very small scale and farmers did not want slaves who required maintenance. The same held true for small craftsmen. If any of these

70, 71 Left, a slave being punished and (right) a young slave with a lantern leading his drunken master home after a party. Though masters had absolute power over their slaves, enlightened Greek opinion insisted on their right to fair treatment.

owned a slave, he might use him for both domestic and business purposes.

The most frequent practice was to hire slaves, who usually received the same pay as a free man. The building industry, for example, hired slaves or free men according to the available manpower. The building accounts of the Erechtheum on the Athenian acropolis list thirty-five marble-workers, of whom twenty-five were slaves and ten were free men; all were paid equally. Because of the practice of slave-hiring and because masters often allowed slaves to run their own businesses, the slave was in some ways in a similar position to the hired worker and small craftsman, but he had to give his master a portion of his income. Consequently, although slavery was an important part of the Athenian economy and society, it was not absolutely essential. If the slaves had been freed *en masse* Athens would have functioned economically much the same. Socially, much domestic inconvenience would have been created, especially for the wealthier, but hired servants would probably have replaced household slaves. The freed slaves would probably have continued to practise their professions, as many of those who had been freed did. Moreover, there must have been a large part of the population which had no domestic slaves. If 25 per cent of the population were slaves, we can subtract the mine slaves and those in the crafts from this number and estimate that perhaps only one household in two or three possessed a domestic slave. Mining was the one area which would have suffered severely from a mass emancipation. Without slave labour its costs would have soared and its continued operations would have been imperilled.

Manumission was infrequent in the classical period and consequently the number of freedmen was small. If a master gave a slave his freedom, or allowed him to purchase it, he had to replace him. Most manumissions, therefore, came about through personal feelings or the offering of a high manumission price. Those slaves likely to accumulate enough money to purchase their freedom were often the ones operating as independent craftsmen, paying a fixed sum to their master. Since they already had considerable freedom, manumission would give them little material benefit. For the same reasons that metics did not press for citizenship, freedmen also felt that they were not entitled to it. The mine slaves, no doubt, would have snatched at liberation from their oppressive conditions. At the silver-mines at Laurium the shifts were ten hours long, digging was by torchlight and by the fourth century the shafts had reached depths of over three hundred feet, so that life expectancy was short. But the slave miners had no way of accumulating money with which to purchase their freedom.

Slave revolts were rare in classical Greece, though in cities such as Sparta where the serfs (as opposed to slaves) were treated harshly and suffered oppression, revolts were common, but usually unsuccessful. In cities such as Athens the mine slaves were too well controlled for rebellion, while the domestic slave was well treated and would probably not be able to earn a good livelihood if freed.

Despite the fact that Athens became the cultural centre and most powerful state of Greece, she remained like the rest of the cities of Greece basically an agricultural society, at least until the end of the fifth century. Although trade was extensive, it was largely in the hands of non-citizens, and never approached the scale of international trade of the Dutch or British empires. Although Athens produced pottery,

72 Ploughing scene on an early sixth-century Attic vase; notwithstanding the growth of commerce most Greek states retained fundamentally agricultural economies.

metalwork and other items for export, industry, as we have seen, was conducted on a very small scale. Consequently, this limited industrialization did not encourage the development of a middle class, as is the case in societies undergoing industrial revolutions. Corresponding most closely to the modern conception of a middle class was the group which consisted of medium-sized landowners, with a few merchants and craftsmen.

THE BREAKDOWN OF ARISTOCRATIC POWER AND THE RISE OF TYRANNY

Civil war and class struggle in the city state usually arose over the issue of who should have full citizenship rights, particularly the rights to hold offices and to legislate. In practice, partial rights generally meant virtual exclusion from rule. Often the struggle of the lower classes to attain full citizenship rights and participation in government produced internal discord. These internal struggles were concentrated in two main periods. One occurred in the seventh and sixth centuries with the break-up of Greece's agricultural society. The other came in the fifth century, when oligarchs and democrats battled for supremacy. At that time the lower classes gained a share in the rule in many states. The oligarchs attempted, often with success, to restrict citizenship, but the democrats fought back. These struggles produced situations like that at Corcyra, which oscillated between oligarchy and democracy with bloody slaughters along the way, or that at Byzantium, which shifted from oligarchy to democracy and back half a dozen times in the late fifth century. Even Athens, the leading democratic state, became an oligarchy once in the sixth century and, under pressure of war and defeat, twice for brief periods in the fifth century.

We have previously seen that the aristocrats' monopoly of power was based on their possession of land and control of the military machinery. Three factors altered this situation: the increase of population and the resulting colonization and trade, the introduction of a moneyed economy, and the emergence of a new type of war arm, the hoplite phalanx.

In colonization the city state found an answer to the economic problems caused by the increase of population in the eighth and seventh centuries. With colonization went trade, a general increase in prosperity, and a market for goods from other cities and countries. Production became more specialized and increasingly more sensitive to the demands of the market. Inevitably this social and economic disruption caused the breakdown of the static agrarian society. Pottery and other wares were produced in greater quantity; the landless *thetes* could find occupations at sea. It was now possible to acquire wealth in forms other than land, thereby undermining the old aristocratic basis for power.

Trade had another effect on the decline of the aristocrats: it increased the availability of metal. Increased supply decreased cost, so more people could afford armour. Any citizen who could furnish his own armour became a knight regardless of his birth, and with this new status came more political power. The greater supply of metal encouraged and allowed the development of hoplite armour and the hoplite infantryman, which was a major factor in destroying the power of the aristocracy.

The introduction of a moneyed economy in Greece in the seventh century also weakened the old aristocracy. Before money was introduced, if a non-aristocratic landowner produced a surplus there was little he could do with it. He would find it almost impossible to acquire more land. There was no satisfactory way to use his accumulated surplus effectively. If more animals were produced, he did not have the land to maintain them. Perhaps he traded part of his surplus for material objects; he probably ate better – it is difficult to store produce under a mattress. With a moneyed economy, however, he could sell off his surplus each year and gradually accumulate capital. The transformation of an aristocracy of birth to one primarily of wealth, which took place between the seventh and fourth centuries, demonstrates the effects of a moneyed economy. The sixth-century poet Theognis of Megara confirms that the owners of small and middle-sized farms acquired wealth through the introduction of

73, 74 Cheaper metals and frequent wars provided a stimulus to craftsmen in armour all over the Greek world. Above, an Athenian armourer at work in his shop; right, a finely decorated pair of bronze greaves, made in the late sixth century BC.

money and commerce and so broke down class barriers in his complaints that 'money mixes the classes', and 'it is not without reason that men honour you above all, O Plutus [wealth]; for through you the base man becomes noble'.

So long as the military might of the state belonged to the aristocrats, so did the political machinery and the decision as to who should have full citizenship rights. About 700 BC, however, the hoplite phalanx was introduced into Greece, revolutionizing warfare and further destroying aristocratic power. Warfare before the hoplite phalanx was a *mêlée* of individual warriors, engaged in single-combat duels with the enemy. Throughout the *Iliad* Homer narrates one single combat after another, until he comes to the greatest battle of warrior against warrior, the duel of Achilles and Hector before the walls of Troy. Fighting was so disorganized that a warrior would often pause in the middle of a battle to despoil a slain opponent of his armour. Homer reports the death of Archelochos: 'But Polydamas himself avoided dark death . . . and Archelochos, son of Antenor, received the spear, since the immortal gods had doomed his destruction.

It hit him at the joining place of head and neck, at the last vertebra, and cut through both of the tendons, so that the man's head and mouth and nose hit the ground far sooner than did the front of his legs and knees as he fell. . . . There Akamas, bestriding his brother, stabbed the Boeotian Promachos with the spear as he tried to drag off the body.' The object of fighting was to acquire glory and booty in the form of metal, armour and women.

By contrast, the hoplite phalanx was a well-organized weapon of destruction. The soldiers stood with locked shields and lumbered, like a tank bristling with spears, across the field of battle. The old-style army had no hope against its advance. Every state was forced to adopt this new method of fighting or lose its military position. Since the hoplite phalanx had to move like one mass and fight in perfect order, the new system, unlike aristocratic warfare, required constant drilling and training and the participation of many of the citizens. The non-aristocrats had the time and inclination to drill; an ever-growing number now could afford to become soldiers, since an expensive horse was no longer needed and the decreased cost of metal had reduced the price of armour.

75 The hoplite's equipment: breastplate, helmet, bronze shield and short, straight-edged iron sword for close fighting.

Hoplite equipment differed from the old type in several ways. The old-style spear was thrown, after which opposing warriors would close with the sword in individual combat. So in the *Iliad* Hector casts his spear at Achilles, striking his shield, and then 'pulling out the sharp sword that was slung at the hollow of his side, . . . he made a swoop, like a high-flown eagle who launches himself out of the murk of the clouds on to the flat land to catch a tender lamb or a shivering hare; so Hector made his swoop, swinging his sharp sword.' The old-style shield had a single handgrip at the centre and a strap round the neck, so that if the soldier had to run he could move his shield round to protect his back. The hoplite defence armour was much heavier. The main piece was a breastplate of metal, the spear was used for thrusting, and the shield was held with an armband and basically covered only the left side of the body. A soldier's right side was protected by the shield of the man standing on his right. It was essential that the line should stand fast, otherwise the right side would be exposed. Thus a new standard of courage in war developed; to stand fast in the hoplite battle-line. The seventh-century poet Tyrtaeus sings:

> No man proves that he is good in war
> Unless he bravely face the bloody carnage,
>   Standing by the foe to strike him down.
> This is man's excellence and finest guerdon,
>   Fairest glory for the young to win.
> A good for all the city, all the people.
>   When a man stands up in battle's front
> And flinches not, nor thinks of base withdrawal,
>   But sets heart and spirit to endure,
> And with his words makes brave the man beside him:
>   So the good man is revealed in war.

(tr. C. M. Bowra)

In flight the shield offered no protection and the hoplite could throw it away. The poet Archilochus, attacking the aristocratic values of courage, wrote, 'Some Saian rejoices in my shield. Though I did not want to, I left it, blameless, by a bush. And I myself fled death. To hell with that shield. I'll get another just as good.'

Aristotle argued that the earliest constitutions were narrow because the early Greek states based their military power on the cavalry and only the wealthy could afford horses. With the hoplite, however, the military power base was widened and the hoplites demanded and obtained a greater share in ruling the state. In Athens the acquisition of full rights of citizenship went together with military contribution to the state. Aristocrats had full power while they controlled the military forces; the moderate- and small-sized farmers acquired rights only when they became the military bulwark of the state as hoplites. The lowest class of citizens, the *thetes*, gained nearly full rights in Athens by the end of the fifth century, when they were needed to row the ships on which the supremacy of the city depended.

During the seventh and sixth centuries, when aristocratic power was disintegrating, disruption and class struggle boiled within Greek cities. Amid these upheavals tyrants emerged in many places. They were autocrats but not necessarily despots. They often passed on their power to their sons, but the tyranny seldom survived for more than two or three generations, mainly because the unstable conditions which created it soon passed. The tyrants often indirectly contributed to their own downfall, since by their policies they broke the power of the aristocrats and encouraged the rise in that of the hoplites and the commercially oriented classes at the expense of the aristocrats. As these new segments became stronger they would no longer tolerate rule by tyrants as a substitute for constitutionally delegated power. Thus Greek tyranny, for the most part, marks a short transitional stage from aristocracy to new forms of government – oligarchy and democracy.

The reasons for the imposition of a tyranny varied from state to state, but it is no coincidence that tyranny arose in Greece within a short time of the introduction of the hoplite. Some tyrants, such as Peisistratus of Athens, were military leaders before becoming tyrants. The events at Corinth illustrate well the importance of the hoplite and the tyrant's rule in the breakdown of aristocratic power. Corinth had been ruled by the aristocratic clan of the Bacchiads. Under their influence, in the late eighth century Corinth greatly expanded her western trade. The Bacchiads founded the two important western colonies of Syracuse and Corcyra; they also stimulated trade, which increased the prosperity of Corinth. In the process, however, they fostered the creation of a new moneyed class and the disintegration of the old balanced agricultural society. Dissatisfaction grew as the Bacchiads became less successful in their foreign and economic policies at the end of the eighth century. Their rule became more restrictive, and they were eventually overthrown by Cypselus.

76 A review of the Attic cavalry in the early fifth century. The importance of cavalry, an aristocratic prerogative, declined with the rise of the hoplite, who in most Greek armies soon outnumbered cavalrymen ten to one.

Herodotus records his rise to power, embellishing his account with a folk motif which is also found in the stories of Perseus, Cyrus and Moses. Cypselus' mother, Labda, was a Bacchiad who had married outside the clan, since her lameness made her unattractive as a bride to anyone within it. On Cypselus' birth the Bacchiads resolved to kill him, owing to some unfavourable oracles; but his mother hid him from them in a chest (*kypsele*) from which he derived his name. When he grew up he seized power and set himself up as tyrant. Although the evidence is scanty, the hoplites were probably his main supporters, with assistance from the new rich. He apparently held the post of polemarch or war-leader before becoming tyrant. This and the fact that once in power he never needed a bodyguard suggest that the army was on his side.

In the cases of Athens and Sparta more evidence is available for the importance of the new classes and the hoplites in the internal struggles of the seventh and sixth centuries. Sparta, as we have seen, managed to avoid a tyranny by her adoption of the Lycurgan system. Defeated by neighbouring Argos at Hysiae in 669 BC, she was temporarily halted in her expansion in the Peloponnese, and within a short time of this reversal a major Messenian revolt occurred on the heels of local wars with Argos, Arcadia and Elis. The ineffectiveness of the aristocratic government, together with the ravages of war, induced the Spartan hoplites to call for a redistribution of land. Instead of meeting this demand 'Lycurgus' increased the hoplites' political rights and made them 'equals'. He also reorganized Sparta's military and political machinery. The army was henceforth based on locality instead of tribe; the size of the council was fixed; an assembly was to be formed of nine thousand 'equals'. As in the rest of Greece, the council would make proposals for confirmation by the assembly, but in Sparta the council could disregard the assembly if it spoke 'with a crooked voice'. The Lycurgan system stabilized Spartan society, and through it the Spartan aristocracy survived a crisis of a kind which led to tyranny in other states. To some extent they did this by satisfying the demands of the hoplites and creating a hoplite constitution. Military reforms as a peaceful solution to revolution enabled Sparta to gain dominance over other states in the sixth and fifth centuries. The system was initially so efficient in enabling Sparta to control her helots that its abandonment would have meant the loss of Laconia; but it was not flexible enough to admit of fruitful alteration.

Discontent among Sparta's citizen population after the mid-seventh century was minimal. Power struggles certainly occurred, but at no time did civil war erupt among the citizens, as it did in most cities of Greece. Civil war would have destroyed Sparta, since it would have given the helots an opportunity for successful revolt. Thus the militaristic society which Sparta created had to stand united against the ever-present helot menace. For civil war between different sections of society, however, Sparta exchanged helot revolts. With a hostile and enslaved population, internal harmony in Sparta was nearly impossible, although the *status quo* could be maintained.

The situation in Athens provides a more complete picture of the breakdown of aristocratic power and the struggles of the classes. In the late 630s BC an aristocrat named Cylon, supported by his father-in-law, the tyrant of Megara, attempted to set up a tyranny in Athens. At that period Athens was still ruled by its aristocrats (called the 'Eupatrids', the 'well-born'). Cylon with the aid of Megarian troops seized the acropolis, but Megacles, the archon, apparently with popular support, led a counter-attack and defeated the invaders, forcing them to take sanctuary in the Temple of Athena. Promised their lives if they surrendered, however, Cylon and his supporters left their refuge, only to be led away and put to death. Cylon probably failed through lack of public support, which suggests that discontent was not widespread. Yet there must have been some friction in the city for Cylon even to have considered making his attempt. Aristocratic strife certainly existed, for the aristocrats combined against Megacles and his clan, the Alcmaeonids (which was to supply many of Athens' future radical leaders, among them Cleisthenes and Pericles), secured their exile and had them cursed by the Delphic Oracle, ostensibly for their execution of Cylon. According to Plutarch, even the bodies of dead Alcmaeonids were disinterred and cast out beyond the borders of the country.

Aristotle remarks that 'afterwards [i.e. after Cylon] for a long time civil struggles took place between the nobles and the people.' Within a few years of Cylon's attempt at tyranny a certain Draco published the first law code in Athens. We can deduce that there must have been some undercurrent of discontent before it, since codes of law are usually promulgated as a means of settling disputes and clearly defining citizens' rights. Such was the case with the Twelve Tables in Rome and Solon's legal code, which was formulated in Athens a few decades after Draco's. Little is known about Draco's laws except that they gained a reputation for severity. According to Plutarch, they were written not in ink but in blood. When asked why he made death the penalty for most crimes, Draco was said to have replied that the lesser ones deserved it and no more severe penalty could be found for the greater ones. An enlightened part of the code, however, was Draco's distinction between murder and manslaughter.

By 594 BC Athens had reached a state of crisis. Civil war or tyranny was imminent. All elements of society were at odds, the poor, the rich, the hoplites, the aristocrats. Two main problems faced the city, an economic one and a political one. The new rich, many of whom were hoplites, were agitating for a greater share in the rule of the state and increased rights, as were the hoplites as a group. Through debt many small farmers had fallen into a serf-like condition called 'hectemorage', and still others into slavery. The *hectemoros* was required to give one-sixth of his produce to his creditor, usually a rich landowner. If he failed in this obligation, as he might in a poor year when he needed his whole crop to keep from starving, he and his family had to pay by their own enslavement. Tenant farming, or sharecropping, probably arose through loans made to the small farmer, and was not, in fact, uncommon in the Mediterranean. It occurred, for example, in Egypt: 'Joseph told the people, "Now that I have acquired you and your land for Pharaoh, here is seed for you to sow

77, 78 The first coins to be struck to a specific standard were those of the kingdom of Lydia. Left, sixth-century Lydian gold stater of the reign of Croesus; right, Milesian electrum coin of *c.* 575 BC.

the land. But when the harvest is in, you must give a fifth to Pharaoh, keeping four-fifths as seed for yourselves, as food for yourselves and members of your households, and to feed the children'' (Genesis 47).

The small farmer was driven into debt for several reasons, the most important of which was the changing economic situation. The growth of trade and commerce in the eighth and seventh centuries had disrupted Greece's agrarian economy. Coinage was introduced to Greece in the seventh century. As we have noted, coinage and the ability to store wealth helped weaken aristocratic power, but it also contributed to the indebtedness of the small farmer. The Greeks dealt by barter until, in the eighth and seventh centuries, trade brought them into contact with the more sophisticated Near East, where precious metals such as gold and silver had long been used in commerce. Near Eastern governments did not mint fixed units of coinage, however; instead, traders would weigh out amounts at each transaction. The Greeks, for their part, sometimes used an iron currency, which took the form of iron utensils, such as tripods or weapons. Later the iron 'spit' was used as a more standardized measure.

At times various Near Eastern states guaranteed the standard of precious metals, but they did not issue coins until the Lydians began the practice in the seventh century. The basic concept behind the issuing of coinage is that in placing its stamp on a coin a state thereby guarantees the purity and weight. Although the first coins were not struck in Greece until the last quarter of the seventh century, the use of precious metals in trade and of primitive iron currency encouraged the rapid and widespread adoption of coinage.

Expanding trade and commerce and the introduction of coinage deeply affected economic conditions. All segments of society were able to benefit save the peasant, whose condition must have been exacerbated by these changes. The aristocracy encouraged trade and through it many earned fortunes. By means of coinage the middle-sized landowners were able to accumulate wealth, but the poor suffered, since products increased in price, especially those for which there was a market abroad. They could not easily switch to the cultivation of those goods which fetched the best prices, since these required a certain investment. It takes well over a dozen years for an olive tree to grow sufficiently to bear fruit, and from three to four years for vines to produce grapes. A farmer who has near subsistence level could not afford to set aside part of his land for these new crops since he might starve in the meantime. Thus society became stratified into the very rich, the very poor, the new commercial class and the hoplites.

Amidst this turmoil arose the figure of Solon. He was an Athenian aristocrat of the old royal Medontid clan, but his allegiance was not to the aristocrats. Part of his life he spent as a merchant, and in 594 BC he came to power in Athens as a mediator. He stood on the side of the poor against the aristocrats, but he was by no means a radical, rather a patriotic Athenian who tended towards a moderate conservativism. Fortunately for historians he wrote many poems on the crisis, some of which are extant. After reading all the poems Aristotle concluded that Solon had laid the blame for Athens' troubles squarely on the shoulders of the rich. He had attacked the rich for their greed, which caused slavery in the city and 'which is rousing up civil strife and sleeping war'. Solon classed himself with the poor, as is shown by his verses: 'for many base men are rich and many noble poor, but we will not exchange our virtue for their wealth.'

As mediator and lawgiver, Solon instituted reforms in the economic, social and political spheres. His first problem was that of the poor farmer, the *hectemoros*. In an Act called *seisachtheia*, or 'shaking off of burdens', Solon cancelled their debts. He forbade all further loans on the security of the person and abolished hectemorage. He also re-purchased Athenians who had been sold as slaves abroad and returned them to Athens. He himself boasted of having freed the land by picking up the *horoi*, which were planted everywhere. *Horoi* were probably markers which showed that the land on which they stood was mortgaged.

Solon cannot have cancelled all debts in his reforms. To do so would have destroyed the economic fabric of Athenian society. So far as day-to-day living was concerned the amount of debt was low. Coinage had just been introduced and the small denominations of coins required for daily business were at this time virtually non-existent. A farmer who bought an amphora from a potter would have to pay in merchandise or possibly with iron 'spits'; he would not be billed. Major debts probably took one of two main forms, mortgages on land or debts connected with shipping. Aristocrats usually became involved in trade as investors rather than as individual merchants. Bottomry loans were, as we have seen, not uncommon, and many routine debts would be incurred in the trading business. Solon particularly wished to encourage trade and commerce, a desire indicated by such parts of his legislation as the bestowal of full citizenship on foreign craftsmen who would migrate to Athens: we have evidence of Corinthian potters who took up this offer and thus gave new impetus to the Athenian pottery industry. Solon also modified the weights and coinage system and regulated exports and imports, especially by his prohibition of the export of any agricultural

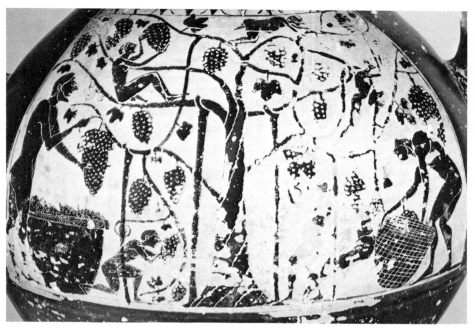

79–82 Olive oil and wine have been among the principal agricultural products of Greece in all periods. Above, sixth-century representations of the olive harvest and of grape-picking. Left, part of an olive-press from Delos; below, a Cypriote vase depicting the export of oil or wine.

product save oil. Olive oil was a particularly important product in the Mediterranean, where animal fats were scarce. It served as a lubricant, took the place of soap and butter, and provided fuel for lamps. Thus Solon's stimulation of trade and commerce suggests that *seisachtheia* most likely applied only to land debts.

Although we do not have direct evidence of strong agitation for citizenship rights, Solon's constitutional reforms show that part of the crisis was due to a demand for full citizen rights and the ability to participate in government. Among the most important features of Solon's legislation in this sphere was his division of the citizens into four classes, the *pentakosiomedimnoi* or five-hundred-bushel men, the *hippeis* or knights, the *zeugitai* or yoke-men, and the *thetes*. Since the use of cavalry was minimal, the *hippeis* were knights virtually in name only. They usually served as hoplites along with the *zeugitai*, who comprised the bulk of the hoplite group. Aristotle writes that the class divisions were made according to the income a man obtained from his own property: respectively five hundred, three hundred and two hundred *medimnoi* of dry and liquid produce for the top three classes. These must have been only rough estimates: production might vary from year to year and it would be impossible to keep re-evaluating the worth of individuals. Wealth from trade and commerce and other material wealth not connected with land must also have been taken into account, for Solon was certainly not going to discourage trade by debarring those whose wealth derived from it from achieving the appropriate class and social status.

The importance of this reform lay in the concomitant rights which accompanied class status. All *pentakosiomedimnoi* were eligible to become chief officials, such as archon and treasurer, regardless of their birth. The aristocracy's stranglehold on the government was gone, though not its dominance. The new class of wealthy non-aristocrats had gained a share in the rule. The higher offices, except those of treasurer and archon, were open to the knights as well. Solon admitted the *zeugitai* to lesser offices and allowed the *thetes* to be members of the assembly. Since the assembly elected the officials, even the *thetes* thus had a voice in naming the chief of state, though they themselves could not stand for office.

Solon is said to have instituted the Council of the Four Hundred, consisting of one hundred members from each tribe, probably to be chosen from the top three classes. This new council was to serve a 'probouleutic' function, that is, to prepare legislation to be voted upon by the *ecclesia* or assembly. In instituting this new council Solon diminished the power of the aristocratic council, the Areopagus, which was composed of ex-archons. Since the newly wealthy could now hold the archonship, they could henceforth become members of the Areopagus, but in 594 BC the Areopagus was entirely composed of the old aristocracy and it would be many years before the newly wealthy could gain an adequate representation, especially since its members served for life and the newly wealthy might not be elected every year.

Similar economic and political problems and the class struggles which ensued were resolved in other states at this time by tyranny. This turn of events was prevented in Athens because of Solon's administrative skill and his unwillingness to become a tyrant himself. He comments in his verses that, although certain factions urged him to become tyrant, he had refused: 'for once I had seized power, gained infinite wealth, been tyrant of Athens even for one day, I would have been ready to be flayed for a wineskin and my family to be wiped out.' The class which most urged this course upon him must have been the hoplites. The *thetes* were somewhat satisfied when hectemorage was eliminated. The wealthy commoners had gained a share in the government as five-hundred-bushel men and knights. The *zeugitai*, the less affluent of the hoplites, had gained least, although there was some rumble of discontent in all classes since the lower classes felt that Solon had not gone far enough and the upper that he had gone too far.

Thus Solon's economic and political reforms averted the crisis at Athens without civil war or tyranny – but only temporarily, for within thirty years class conflict again flared up, this time resulting in a tyranny. That Solon's reforms had only temporary success was mainly due to his failure to break the power of the old aristocrats. Although the new rich had been admitted to higher offices, the old aristocracy still retained much of its power. It continued to control the tribal and religious organizations and to possess much political influence. The general pattern in Greece was for a tyrant to emerge with the support of the new rich and hoplites, and to pit himself against the old aristocracy, whose power he eventually undermined or destroyed. For the same result to be achieved in Athens a tyrant was needed. This man was to be Peisistratus, who crushed the power of the old landed aristocrats and thereby paved the way for the establishment of democracy under Cleisthenes.

His reforms enacted, Solon left Athens to travel for ten years, after first making the Athenians swear to make no changes in the law during his absence. 'He did not wish to have to interpret the laws himself', Aristotle says, '. . . but every citizen should obey them according to what was written.' Minor struggles erupted almost immediately, probably because of aristocratic opposition to the new class divisions. Of the next fifteen years two were *anarchiae* (without archons) and one man, Damasias, held the archonship illegally for two years from 582 to 580 BC. When Damasias was deposed a compromise was reached with nobles and non-nobles sharing the office.

The aristocrats, however, prevented any further diminution of their power and by the 560s two major factions had become prominent in the struggle for power, the aristocratic party of the Plain, led by Lycurgus, and the more moderate party of the Coast, led by Megacles, an Alcmaeonid. According to Herodotus, Peisistratus then formed a third party, the *hyperakrioi* or 'men beyond the hills', with the intention of making himself tyrant. Peisistratus had an indomitable drive to become tyrant. It took him three attempts over fifteen years before he had securely established himself. His first try came in 561 BC. Wounding himself, he claimed he had been attacked by his enemies and thus persuaded the assembly to allow him to have a bodyguard, which, though armed only with clubs, proved sufficiently strong to allow him to seize the acropolis and make himself tyrant. This action induced Megacles and Lycurgus to combine forces to expel him. On Peisistratus' exit, however, the temporary alliance between Megacles and Lycurgus collapsed and their feuding re-ignited. Megacles, fearing defeat, allied himself with his recent enemy Peisistratus and plotted to return him as tyrant. Their plan seems naïve, but its success shows that they understood the Athenian mind better than Herodotus, who was incredulous at the stupidity of the Athenian people in this matter, if indeed the story has any truth to it. An unnaturally tall girl by the name of Phya is said to have been dressed up as Athena, and to have led Peisistratus back to the acropolis, while his adherents proclaimed that the goddess Athena herself was returning Peisistratus to power. The Athenians were probably not so gullible as Herodotus imagines. Undoubtedly the coalition of Peisistratus' and Megacles' factions alone was sufficient to restore the former to power. The Phya episode was probably propaganda to give Peisistratus a moral claim to rule. The alliance between Peisistratus and Megacles was sealed by the marriage of Megacles' daughter to

Peisistratus, a seal that was soon broken. Either because he wished to avoid producing offspring or through unnatural proclivities, however, Peisistratus slept with his wife 'contrary to custom'. When her father found out, the fragile alliance of Peisistratus and Megacles was at an end and Peisistratus again found himself an exile.

This time Peisistratus resolved to establish his position on a firmer basis and never go on his travels again. Using Eretria as a base, he spent the next ten years consolidating his power by acquiring wealth from the Thracian silver-mines and securing the support of foreign allies, especially Argos (whence his second wife had come). About 546 BC he landed near Marathon at the head of an army of foreign soldiers, mostly mercenaries. Joined by his supporters from Athens, he fought a victorious battle at Pallene which re-established his tyranny. The remainder of his reign was peaceful and successful, both politically and economically. He died in 527 BC and was succeeded by his son Hippias and Hipparchus, who ruled as tolerant moderates until the murder of Hipparchus in 514 BC at the hands of Harmodius and Aristogeiton. Thereafter Hippias' rule became harsher, and in 510 BC he was expelled by the Alcmaeonid clan, aided by Sparta.

The key to the civil strife which brought Peisistratus to power lies in the failure of Solon's reforms to endure and in the nature of the three political factions. That Megacles could ally himself first with Lycurgus and then with Peisistratus, while Peisistratus and Lycurgus never joined forces, suggests that Megacles led the moderate faction, while Lycurgus and Peisistratus stood at the extremes of right and left respectively. According to Aristotle Lycurgus' party was oligarchic, Megacles' moderate and Peisistratus had the support of the people. The three parties may have had some regional associations, as their names imply. The party of the Plain is usually thought to have been composed of the old landowning aristocrats, especially since Lycurgus himself probably belonged to an old aristocratic family. The party of the Coast is considered to have been the party of the commercial class and the *nouveaux riches*, while the *hyperakrioi* represented the small farmers and the urban poor. The party names probably arose because of local support for the leaders in those areas. Peisistratus himself came from Brauron, some distance from the city, but much of his power stemmed from the city mob. The old aristocracy was spread throughout the country and not confined to the plain, nor the new rich to the coast.

Until the appearance of Peisistratus, the struggle had been between the party of the Coast, the newly admitted citizens, and the party of the Plain, the old land-holding aristocrats. Peisistratus may have represented the hoplite class as well as the poorer farmers and city mob. Like some other tyrants he had military connections. Before he came to power he had been general in the war against the Megarians and had seized their harbour of Nisaea. When he first took power by force he apparently encountered no armed opposition, a fact which indicates that he had the support, or at least the acquiescence, of the hoplites. His return for the second time to the tyranny was likewise without armed opposition, while on his third seizure of power his followers flocked from Athens to fight at his side. The battle of Pallene was such a one-sided affair that he may well have had Athenian hoplite assistance for his mercenary forces. On the other hand, Peisistratus cannot have had the undivided loyalty of the hoplites or he would not have been driven out initially. According to ancient sources the poor and the city mob, the disenfranchised and those who had not benefited from Solon's reforms were Peisistratus' supporters.

Megacles, the leader of the party of the Plain, was of the Alcmaeonid clan, an aristocrat, but with traditionally strong liberal leanings. His grandfather of the same name had thwarted Cylon's attempt at tyranny. Megacles wed Agariste of Sicyon and had a son whom he named Cleisthenes, after his father-in-law. This Cleisthenes was to be the great liberal who established the democracy after the expulsion

83–86 Peisistratus' régime brought many civic improvements to Athens, notably an increased water-supply. Opposite, scene at a water-fountain on a late sixth-century Attic vase. Above, the remains of the Enneakrounos fountain-house built by Peisistratus and the drain-pipes that ran through the Athenian agora to supply it; right, a marker which served to delineate its boundary.

of Hippias, the son of Peisistratus. Megacles' party was composed of the wealthy merchants, members of the commercial class and the new rich who had been enfranchised by Solon. Until Peisistratus appeared on the scene their struggle had been against the old landed aristocrats, and undoubtedly in creating his new party Peisistratus took with him the left-wing elements of Megacles' party.

Peisistratus did not alter Solon's constitution once in power. His mercenaries guaranteed his rule, and he maintained power through the installation of his followers in political offices. This method was followed by Peisistratus' sons, who placed their political henchmen in the office of archon. The archon list survives for the years from 528 to 521 BC. Peisistratus died in 528/527 BC, and in 526/525 Hippias, Peisistratus' son, was archon. He was followed by Cleisthenes, Miltiades, Calliades and Hippias' son, also called Peisistratus. Ostensibly Peisistratus was a private citizen. Once he was even summoned before the Areopagus on the charge of homicide; but when the tyrant appeared in person to defend himself the man who had brought the charge for some reason failed to appear.

When Peisistratus regained control of Athens after the battle of Pallene in 546 BC, the city had suffered fifteen to twenty years of party and class strife. Peisistratus sought at once to conciliate all factions, and in this he skilfully succeeded. According to Aristotle 'the majority both of the nobles and the common people were in his favour. The former he won over by diplomacy and the latter by the help which he gave them in their private affairs; and he always proved fair to both of them.'

He sought to help the small farmer and urban proletariat. Taxing agricultural produce at the rate of either 5 or 10 per cent, he then returned part of the money to the small farmers in the form of loans, possibly to help them convert from wheat production to the cultivation of the vine and olive. Government loans to the small farmers transferred their primary obligation, away from the nobles from whom they had previously borrowed, to the state. The produce tax gave the government a steady source of income, much of which was also channelled back into the economy in the form of public works, such as the building of temples and fountains. Peisistratus' building programme and public works, among them the construction of the Temple of Athena Parthenos on the acropolis, the start of the building of the great Temple of Olympian Zeus and the erection of the fountain-house Enneakrounos, or 'Nine Springs', all helped to

87 Dionysus: Peisistratus' promotion of the worship of this originally
rustic god at Athens helped to unite urban and rural elements in Attic society.

make the city of Athens the centre of Attica and at the same time to spread the new wealth of the state among the populace by providing a steady source of employment for skilled and unskilled workers, particularly the urban poor.

By the end of the sixth century and the beginning of the fifth, the Attic farmer primarily cultivated the vine and olive and was fairly prosperous, a situation for which Peisistratus bears much of the credit. As the domestic grain supply decreased, Peisistratus was compelled to increase Athenian control over foreign grain. In order to secure the lifeline to the vital grain supplies produced in the Black Sea region, Peisistratus first supported Lygdamis in his bid for the tyranny of the island of Naxos. He then retook Sigeum and made his son Hegesistratus ruler, while Miltiades the elder occupied the Thracian Chersonese, giving Athens effective control of the Hellespont and the sailing routes from the Black Sea.

Generally during his reign Peisistratus was conciliatory towards the nobles. Although he took hostages from some of them, hostages

88 Naked woman, probably a maenad, holding an outsize phallos of the sort which may have been carried in Dionysiac processions. Fertility figured largely among Dionysus' many attributes.

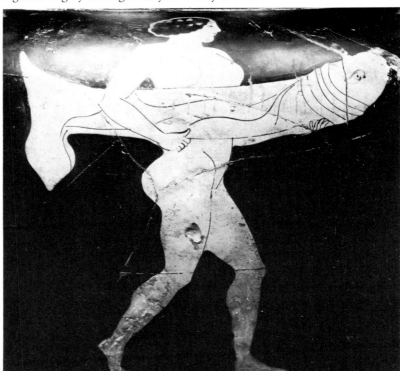

whom he sent to Lygdamis for safekeeping, and although he confiscated the land of some of his opponents who had died at Pallene and of others whom he exiled, his chief method of breaking the power of the old landed aristocracy was not through the confiscation of property or intimidation, but through the strengthening of the central government, which he achieved in many areas, legal, financial, religious and political. He deprived the old clans of some of their privileges, such as the right to mint coins, at the same time improving the coinage and increasing the amount in circulation. He also appointed local judges and travelled about himself on inspection tours, thus diminishing the legal authority of the clans.

Peisistratus attempted to unify the state through religion. He fostered the worship of Demeter, Dionysus and Athena. The first *telesterion* at Eleusis, the centre of the Mystery cult, was built by him. He also purified the sanctuary of Apollo at Delos. But most important were his development of the Great Panathenaea into a major religious festival and his inauguration of the Great Dionysia. Peisistratus attempted to make the Panathenaea, which was celebrated every four years in honour of Athena, a rival to the Panhellenic festivals at Olympia, Corinth and Delphi. This festival brought money into the city, and foreign visitors to be fed and housed. The prizes for the games, Panathenaic amphoras, helped the pottery trade and served as advertisements for Athenian wares abroad. The works of Homer were recited at the festival and there is even a story, probably false, of a Peisistratid recension of the *Iliad* and *Odyssey*. The Great Dionysia admirably served Peisistratus' ends of reconciling the diverse elements of the population. Dionysus was an agrarian god of wine, music and fertility, and this annual festival in his honour helped to bridge the gap between the rural and urban segments of society. The festival also prompted the development of Greek tragedy. Choruses usually sang at it, and in 534 BC Thespis wrote a play for it which introduced an actor as a supplement to the chorus. This is generally considered to be the first tragedy. Within seventy years Aeschylus and Sophocles were writing their great dramas.

Peisistratus and his sons invited craftsmen to Athens and created new citizens from their ranks, as well as conferring citizenship on some of their own supporters. Other Greek tyrants also used the bestowal of citizenship as a means of cementing their power. Gelon of Syracuse was said to have granted Syracusan citizenship to over ten thousand of his mercenaries. Possibly Peisistratus gave full citizenship to some aliens as well as to native Athenians who had only partial or no citizenship rights. The introduction of new citizens further broke down the power of the clans, since previously citizenship had been tightly bound to membership in a specific clan. The new citizens had to be made clan members and this would have diminished the clan's solidarity. Because the old aristocrats dominated the clan, the diminution of its importance likewise diminished aristocratic power.

Peisistratus had found Athens a small city; he left it a major metropolis. While the new prosperity and centralization broke the power of the old landed aristocracy almost completely, it increased the power and political importance of the new rich, and to some extent of the hoplite and lower classes. During the tyranny class struggles all but ceased. The mere existence of a tyrant meant that political wrangling between the aristocratic clans and the classes was unavailing. The lower classes were supported by Peisistratus and thus had little reason to oppose his régime. The only undercurrent of trouble was the aristocratic opposition to the tyranny. With the end of the tyranny, however, the political spectrum polarized into the right, the oligarchs, and the left, the democrats. As in many societies, when the old aristocracy of birth declined it merged with the new non-noble wealthy. These together with the wealthier part of the hoplite class formed the core of the oligarchs. The democrats tended to be the poor, the landowners of medium-sized holdings, and the less successful members of the commercial and hoplite classes.

Often, however, individual members of the aristocracy allied themselves with the lower classes and democratic factions, adopted their political philosophy and became their leaders. The most powerful democratic leaders of fifth-century Athens, such men as Pericles and Alcibiades, were often aristocrats by birth and class. At times popular support was purchased by such means as lavish productions of choruses at festivals by aristocrats with either oligarchic or democratic leanings. But even though individual aristocrats could still dominate the state politically in this way, either in oligarchies or in democracies, their stranglehold on power was gone; they could topple from power, especially in democracies, at the whim of the populace. Even the great Athenian statesman Pericles was tried and convicted on trumped-up charges and deposed from office in 430 BC because the Athenians were dissatisfied with the progress of the Peloponnesian War. For the century following the rule of Peisistratus the struggle in Athens centred on the question of who should have full citizenship rights, which meant who should rule. On one side were the democrats and on the other the oligarchs.

Tyranny served as the transitional phase from the old aristocratic government in Greece to the new constitutions of the classical period, oligarchy and democracy. The class struggles were, however, by no means at an end with this development, but rather became exacerbated. The great rivalry and finally war between Athens and Sparta became an ideological clash between democracy and oligarchy which involved most of Greece. The internal struggle between the systems, begun in Athens with the fall of the tyrant Hippias, continued throughout the fourth century. Among the most stable governments were Athens and Sparta. Athens suffered three brief oligarchies in 510–508, 411/410 and 404/403 BC, while Sparta remained an oligarchy throughout. However, smaller states were not so fortunate, especially during the Peloponnesian War, since both Athens and Sparta fostered democracies and oligarchies respectively in the states which they endeavoured to control.

THE CONFLICT BETWEEN OLIGARCHY AND DEMOCRACY

The fifth century saw the greatest period of internal disunity and civil war in the Greek city states. The oligarchs tried to restrict citizenship to a few, and the democrats to extend it to a wider segment of the population. Oligarchy and democracy were identical in that both limited citizenship and in both the state was ruled only by those with full citizenship rights. But oligarchy was more restrictive and based its exclusions primarily on wealth and the ownership of land. Democracy could also, however, exclude some from full citizenship by virtue of wealth: in Athens, for example, members of the *zeugitai* class were barred from holding the highest offices until the middle of the fifth century. Both systems systematically excluded foreigners, slaves and freemen from citizenship and allowed citizenship with only partial rights to the landless at times and to women and children always.

Although democrats and oligarchs cannot strictly be divided along simple lines of wealth and class, these were important factors. The conflict between them contained many elements of a class struggle. The oligarchs usually came from the wealthier elements of society and the democrats from the poorer. Aristotle, indeed, maintained that the distinction between oligarchy and democracy was simply that between wealth and poverty. If the rulers governed by virtue of their wealth, the system was an oligarchy in his view, even if the rich constituted a majority in the state; the government was labelled a democracy when the poor were masters of the constitution. The oligarchs regarded democracy as a system where the poor exploited the rich; the democrats held a converse view of oligarchy. An oligarchic pamphleteer of the fifth century commented tersely on Athenian democracy: 'The Athenians in my opinion are entitled to little commendation for having originally adopted their present political institutions because they are calculated to give an undue ascendancy to the poor and the bad over the rich and the good.'

As we have noted, the oligarchs were by and large a mixture of the old aristocracy, the new rich, and the more prosperous of the hoplite class, while the democratic faction consisted mainly of the poorer hoplites, the poor peasants and the *thetes*. The hoplite group stood in the middle and, though it tended to favour democracies, it would often support oligarchies instead. The class lines behind the party struggles were not rigidly drawn. But while many individual aristocrats were members of the democratic faction, and many of the poor preferred oligarchy, a poor non-aristocrat would rarely be socially acceptable to the wealthier of the oligarchs – though there were exceptions, such as Socrates.

The oligarchic-democratic struggle over citizenship and the right to participate in government, then, produced internal disunity in many Greek city states. At times the conflicts exploded into civil war. Party strife was continual. The two factions clashed over control of the assemblies, fought in the courts, exiled their opponents, and when necessary assassinated them. Betrayal of cities was common, for the struggle transcended state boundaries. The oligarchs at Athens often felt more loyalty to the oligarchs at Sparta than to a democratic régime at Athens. Democrats in one city would call on democrats of another, even if that city were hostile, for aid against their oligarchs. The same was true of the oligarchs. Thus internal civil strife was often complicated by foreign intervention. This was especially true during the Peloponnesian War, when Greece was divided into two power blocs. Commenting on the bloody civil wars in Corcyra, Thucydides observed that this was the first revolution that occurred, and that afterwards the whole Greek world was convulsed, since in each state the democrats were at variance with the oligarchs, the former trying to bring in the Athenians and the latter the Spartans.

With the end of the tyrants' rule in Athens at the close of the sixth century the city was torn by internal struggles and treason in the form of betrayal to foreign powers. The Spartans were anxious to establish a government friendly to them in Athens and they thus aided the exiled Alcmaeonids in expelling the tyrant Hippias, Peisistratus' son. Civil war soon flared up. The opposing factions were led by Isagoras, an oligarchic aristocrat from an old noble family, and Cleisthenes, the son of Megacles and so, of course, an Alcmaeonid. According to Herodotus, when Cleisthenes was getting the worst of the struggle he allied himself with the *demos*, that is 'the people'. Faced with the increasing power of Cleisthenes, Isagoras then sent to Sparta for aid, and, confident that an oligarchy under Isagoras would best serve Spartan interests, Cleomenes, the Spartan king, sent envoys to demand the expulsion of the Alcmaeonids and a large number of other families. As a pretext the Spartans invoked the old curse which had been laid on the Alcmaeonid family after their ancestor Megacles' sacrilegious execution of Cylon in the seventh century. Cleisthenes judiciously withdrew, but Cleomenes invaded Athens with a small force all the same, exiled seven hundred families, and set up an oligarchy under Isagoras and three hundred of his henchmen. In the face of strong resistance, however, Isagoras tried unsuccessfully to dissolve the old Council, after which he seized the acropolis with its partisans. The members of the Council rallied the Athenian people behind them and besieged the acropolis for two days. Cleomenes now had too few troops for any chance of victory, so he negotiated a safe conduct out of the country for himself and his troops and for Isagoras; but he was compelled to abandon the supporters of Isagoras to the tender mercies of the Athenians, who promptly executed them. Cleisthenes and his followers were now able to return to Athens and to resume the reins of power.

Like his father before him, Cleisthenes initially seems to have led the moderate and liberal factions of the aristocrats and the new wealthy. As a result he was able to attract hoplite support and to ally himself with the people. His victory marked the beginning of the period in which the people formed the power base in the state. While for the next hundred years aristocrats continued to lead the state, they had to depend on the *demos* for their power. By the end of the fifth century the *demos* began to produce its own non-aristocratic leaders.

Cleisthenes sought to break what remained of aristocratic power and cement his own. He instituted constitutional reforms to this end and in so doing firmly established the democracy. He divided Attica into three regions, the city, the coast and the inland portion, ignoring the lines of the former three major parties. The local administrative unit became the village or ward, which was called a 'deme': Attica comprised about 170 demes. The demes within each of the three regions were formed into ten groups called *trittyes*. Then one *trittys* was taken from each area and the resulting three combined into a new tribe. This produced ten tribes, each consisting of three *trittyes*. Cleisthenes established a new Council of Five Hundred, made up of fifty men from each tribe. The ten new tribes replaced the four Ionian tribes and the Council of Five Hundred the old Council of Four Hundred, which had been composed of one hundred from each of the four tribes. Cleisthenes did not abolish the older four tribes, but left them their religious and ceremonial functions. The introduction of the deme was a means of giving political focus to the local area, and at the same time of diminishing the importance of the tribe and the phratry. However, a citizen still had to be a member of a phratry and the practice of assigning new citizens to a phratry continued.

Our lack of knowledge of the social and political make-up of the demes leaves us uncertain as to the purpose and result of Cleisthenes' reforms. According to Aristotle the motive behind the tribal reorganization was to smooth the way for the enrolment of new citizens and the imposing of the deme name was a device to obscure the origin of these citizens. Cleisthenes enfranchised large numbers of noncitizens, some of whom had been given citizenship under Peisistratus but had been disenfranchised by Isagoras and his faction following the expulsion of Hippias. According to Aristotle many foreigners and slave metics (i.e. freed slaves with the status of metics) were also admitted to the tribes and, presumably, citizenship. The exclusion of the *thetes* from office, however, continued and the archons were still drawn from the two highest classes.

Although Aristotle's description of the details of Cleisthenes' reforms is thought to be trustworthy, his interpretation of motives is not. The enfranchisement by Cleisthenes of those who had been excluded from citizenship was only incidental to his main reforms. His purpose in rearranging the tribes was apparently to break down the political power of the four old tribes which had been dominated, for the most part, by the aristocrats. To ensure that the new tribes would not fall into the same situation, Cleisthenes divided the tribes so that they did not represent single geographical areas, thus undermining the aristocracy, whose influence was mainly local. While diminishing the power of the other aristocratic clans by his redivision, he simultaneously increased the power of his own clan by gerrymandering. The Alcmaeonids were probably originally settled in the south-west coastal region, but at the time of Cleisthenes branches of the family were located in three different demes of the city area, while an allied family lived in a fourth. Cleisthenes assigned these four demes to four different *trittyes*, but he linked each of these to those coastal *trittyes* which were the old home territory of the Alcmaeonids. The urban *trittys* in which the main branch of the family lived was also joined to the coastal *trittys* where their country home had been. Thus at one stroke Cleisthenes broke down the regional power of the other aristocratic families, while maintaining or perhaps increasing the power of the Alcmaeonids. This is partially demonstrated by the political influence of the Alcmaeonid clan in Athens for the next hundred years, and their frequent success in securing the election of one of their number as general of their tribe.

As a safety-valve to class strife Cleisthenes introduced the institution of ostracism. Once a year the assembly voted on whether or not an ostracism should be held during that year. If the vote was affirmative, there followed an unpopularity contest in which every man wrote down on a piece of pottery (or *ostrakon*) the name of the politician he would most like to see exiled. The man who received the most votes went into exile for ten years without loss of property. This curious system offered a peaceful resolution of party strife, often by the exile of the leader of one faction. Much confusion surrounds the origin of ostracism, since although Cleisthenes is regarded as its founder it was not in fact used until 487 BC, well after Cleisthenes' death. This has led some historians to deny Cleisthenes the credit for it, but he may nevertheless have devised it as a political weapon which he found he did not require during his reign. It was, as it were, a reserve measure to be used as a neutralizer of future party strife. Cleisthenes' success in breaking down aristocratic power, in preventing strife between the oligarchic and democratic factions and in stabilizing the state is attested by the fact that ostracism was not invoked for so long a period after its invention.

Although Cleisthenes succeeded in administering the *coup de grâce* to the power of the old landed aristocrats, society was still polarizing. Now that the *nouveaux riches* had won political rights and power, they were reluctant to see them diminished by allowing the lower classes to gain a share in the government. On the other hand, the lower classes were becoming more affluent and were beginning to contribute heavily to the military strength of the state, and thus throughout the fifth century strove to increase their power.

By the end of Cleisthenes' rule, about 500 BC, the *demos* could claim to be the real ruler of Athens, though led and guided by the aristocrats. The oligarchs were not able to seize power again until 411 BC, and then only under pressure of wartime conditions. The situation remained fluid, however; the ideological clash caused party strife and internal disunity throughout the fifth century, with the oligarchs trying constantly to reduce the number of citizens and the democrats to expand it.

In Athens and elsewhere political clubs began to assume importance about this time. Most of these clubs had oligarchic leanings, but some were in the democratic camp. They were usually small as regards the number of members, were attached to a leader of wealth, and were composed of men of similar age and social status. The clubs probably existed chiefly as social groups before the late sixth century: Plato implies that the majority of citizens were involved in clubs in some way. The clubs conducted social functions such as the holding of drinking parties – it was at one such party in 415 BC that a certain Euphiletus persuaded the members of his oligarchic club to bind themselves together by the commission of a common crime, the mutilation of the city's herms, in which as we have seen Alcibiades was involved. Much political rivalry and strife was fomented by these clubs, working for their various candidates. Members were active in litigation for their comrades, and often manipulated legal machinery on their behalf. Various clubs of the same political colour would combine to form the oligarchic factions. They made their political wishes felt by packing assemblies, circulating pamphlets, canvassing and bribing, colluding with officials, manipulating elections, ostracizing and even assassinating opponents. They formed the basis of the oligarchic resistance to the democrats, and their members were the leaders of future oligarchic revolts.

In Athens after the defeat of Isagoras the oligarchic–democratic struggle only once led to open civil war. The oligarchs were able to gain control of the state in 411/410 BC for a short period, and again in 404/403. In the first instance they were ousted without violence, but in the second there was incredible bloodshed.

When the cause of democratic Athens was faring badly in the later years of the Peloponnesian War, the local oligarchs were able to capitalize on the low morale of the citizenry to seize the reins of

89 Two of the bronze or marble herms which stood in large numbers in the streets and squares of many Greek cities as magically protective devices. Originally representations of Hermes, they were later frequently used as portrait-busts.

power. In 415 BC, as we have seen, Athens launched its Sicilian Expedition, primarily aimed at the conquest of Syracuse, the most powerful Greek state in Sicily. In 413 the campaign ended in disaster with the near-annihilation of the Athenian forces. Syracuse had triumphed through her naval power. With this victory the lowest class at Syracuse gained prestige and power, and within three years the moderate democracy at Syracuse was replaced by a radical democracy. In Athens the opposite happened. The Periclean strategy at the beginning of the Peloponnesian War in 431 had been based on the control of the sea and the abdication of control on land. This had meant that the *thetes*, who as rowers formed the vital backbone of the fleet, assumed an even greater military importance than they had enjoyed in the previous fifty years of Athenian naval supremacy; and the esteem for the services of the hoplite soldier had suffered correspondingly. The *thetes* backed the demagogues and the radical democracy which gave them a louder voice in government. The débâcle at Syracuse, however, dealt a heavy blow to the *thetes* both in numbers and in prestige. In 414 BC Sparta reopened the Peloponnesian War and the next year she first established a permanent base in Attica at Decelea, ravaging the countryside and forcing the Athenian farmers back into the city. The necessity of dealing with enemy forces on land renewed the importance of the hoplites. To complicate matters further, the

143

naval war off the coast of Asia Minor was vigorously renewed by the Spartans in 412 BC and from then until 410 BC many *thetes* of military age were absent from the city. Moreover, the moderate faction which included most of the hoplites had lost their leader Nicias, who had been executed by the Syracusans after his defeat in Sicily.

Conditions were ripe for an oligarchic revolution. A new breed of oligarchs had emerged in the years since the outbreak of the Peloponnesian War. They were no longer arch political and moral conservatives, but had been brought up in the intellectual revolution of the sophists, who turned their attention first to science, then to rhetoric, political theory and philosophy. Although the democrats had also been exposed to sophist teachings and a number were much influenced by them, the impact on them was on the whole considerably weaker. Thus the new oligarch felt himself separated by education as well as by class from the democrats.

In 412/411 BC, Alcibiades, the Athenian general who had deserted Athens for Sparta in 415 and Sparta for Persia in 412, was negotiating with the Athenian oligarchic faction at Samos, the headquarters of the Athenian fleet. He assured them that he could bring the Persians to the Athenian side if Athens changed her government to an oligarchy. Peisander, the oligarch with whom Alcibiades was dealing, returned to Athens and persuaded the assembly to accede to Alcibiades' terms. But Alcibiades was unable to fulfil his promise of Persian support and broke with the oligarchs. By now, however, matters at Athens had gone too far for the oligarchs to be thwarted. By a reign of terror and the murder of several radical democrats, including Androcles their leader, a narrow oligarchy of four hundred seized control of Athens. They were able to do this through the acquiescence of the moderates. Still leaderless, this faction opposed the radical democrats; but they were too disorganized to take any positive action and thus fell in with the oligarchs. The oligarchs maintained that they wished to restore a 'sounder' form of democracy, which meant depriving the lower classes of full rights. Immediately they excluded the *thetes* from the assembly, eliminated pay for state services, except military ones, and limited the citizenship to five thousand men.

Although the oligarchs now controlled Athens, they still had to win the indispensable support of the Athenian navy which was presently stationed on the island of Samos. They therefore incited an oligarchic revolt there, but it failed miserably, partly because of ineptitude and partly because democratic feeling was too strong among the sailors. The navy was eager to sail back to Athens to depose the oligarchs, but realizing that this precipitous action would leave the coast of Asia Minor a prey to Sparta, Alcibiades persuaded the fleet to wait. Without control of the fleet the oligarchs had failed. They were forced to negotiate with Alcibiades, who insisted that the so-called Five Thousand replace the Four Hundred, and that the Council of the Five Hundred be restored. Most of the extremists escaped to Spartan-held Decelea, but two of their leaders, Antiphon and Archeptolemos, remained in Athens, where they were tried and executed. Theramenes, a moderate oligarch, now took charge of the government. The *thetes* were still excluded from the assembly, but all those who could provide hoplite armour were admitted to citizenship: their number amounted to some nine thousand. Since Athens was so dependent on the rowers in the fleet, however, such a situation could not last long. After a decisive naval victory over Sparta at Cyzicus in 410 BC the radical democracy was restored.

The oligarchic revolt of 411 represented the culmination of the class divisions and hatred that had been building up since the outbreak of the Peloponnesian War. After the death of Pericles in 429 the radical democrats had grown increasingly powerful and increasingly radical. Although some of their leaders were still aristocrats, it was not the same breed that had ruled since Cleisthenes, but rather the unrestrained demagogues. We have seen that, throughout the history of Greece, the military contributions of a particular class led to increased political rights for that class. The *thetes* had failed in Sicily and that gave the oligarchs their chance to deprive them of full rights of citizenship and to turn back the clock. The hoplites temporarily backed the oligarchs, yet the oligarchs failed because they could not keep that allegiance, and the state still depended on the *thetes* for military power.

Within six years of the restoration of democracy in 410 BC, however, the destruction of the Athenian fleet at Aegospotami brought an end to the Peloponnesian War and defeat to Athens. Because the war had embodied an ideological struggle between democracy and oligarchy, it was inevitable that in defeat Athens should become an oligarchy. Without the war and without the empire the military value of the *thetes* was nil. Further, their numbers had been depleted by the execution of three thousand of them at the hands of Lysander after the battle of Aegospotami. Under the terms of peace with Sparta no formal provision was made for effecting the change in government. But Theramenes, the moderate oligarch whose diplomacy was partially responsible for the mild terms which Athens had received, probably indicated in private that he would soon bring about the desired shift. Indeed, within a short time, at the unofficial insistence of Lysander and the Spartans, the Athenian assembly voted to form a provisional government under thirty men. This group was called the Thirty, and later the Thirty Tyrants. Theramenes at first maintained control of the Thirty, but he very quickly lost it to Critias, an extreme oligarch who called in a Spartan garrison and began a reign of terror. He drew up a list of three thousand potential supporters of various oligarchic hues who were to have full citizenship rights. Anyone not on the list could be executed by the Thirty without trial. Short of funds, the Thirty now proposed to execute certain rich metics and to confiscate their property. When Theramenes objected, Critias struck his name off the list of the Three Thousand full citizens and ordered his execution. Theramenes was led out through the streets and given the hemlock to drink. As he raised the cup to his lips his final words were 'Here's to the health of my beloved Critias.' With the death of Theramenes the last restraint on the Thirty was removed, and as the reign of terror continued many Athenians fled their homeland.

In the winter of 404/403 BC about seventy Athenian exiles under the democratic leader Thrasybulus returned to Attica from their place of refuge in Thebes, raised a force of nearly a thousand men and marched on the Piraeus, where Critias was slain in the fighting. As opposition to them grew, the Thirty retreated to nearby Eleusis leaving some of their adherents from among the Three Thousand full citizens to take control of Athens, while the opposing forces of Thrasybulus held the Piraeus. Finally, when Thrasybulus began a siege of Athens itself, the Thirty begged for assistance from Sparta. At the urging of Lysander, Sparta sent a fleet to blockade the Piraeus. Lysander himself marched to Eleusis with the intention of attacking the democrats in the Piraeus from there, but at the last moment internal dissension in Sparta thwarted his plan. Many Spartans, especially King Pausanias, felt that Lysander was amassing too much power through his puppet oligarchies in the conquered cities, so Pausanias now led a second Spartan army into Attica to prevent Lysander from gaining firm control of Athens. Pausanias forced a compromise between Athens and the Piraeus, held by the Three Thousand full citizens and the democrats respectively. Since the Three Thousand were nowhere near as extreme in their oligarchic sentiments and most of them were not intimately involved in the vicious and illegal acts of the Thirty even if they strongly supported them, the democrats reluctantly agreed to an amnesty for all except the Thirty themselves and about twenty of their most culpable supporters. Sparta imposed no form of government, but the democrats gained the upper hand. Pausanias was satisfied: although there was no oligarchy in Athens, at least the leaders of that city were no longer loyal to Lysander. The Thirty remained at Eleusis, untouched until 401 BC when they began to hire mercenary troops. At this new threat the democrats marched out against them and, after luring them to a conference, murdered them. They then made peace with those oligarchs who still survived at Eleusis.

Thrasybulus was no politician, and the leadership of the democrats fell to others, Archinus and Anytus. There was a proposal to limit full citizenship to those who owned land, but this measure was defeated. Within a short time many of the Three Thousand were reconciled to the democrats and a moderate democracy emerged under the leadership of Anytus. After years of foreign war, followed by civil war, Athens began to make strides towards recovery.

The extreme oligarchs failed because of their very extremism. If they had allowed a broader oligarchy, like that of the Five Thousand who had ruled under Theramenes' leadership in 410, they could probably have developed an adequate power base among the populace, especially since the *thetes* were no longer of vital military importance. Even after limiting the state to three thousand full citizens they might have been able to govern, had it not been for their self-interested reign of terror in which they struck at personal enemies, concentrated on gaining wealth and completely disregarded the rights of almost all Athenians. Their actions succeeded in turning the entire state, citizens, metics, oligarchs and democrats, against them. The barbarity of the Thirty made Athenians more loyal to the restored democracy than ever before. Even Plato, who had no love for democracy, remarked that the excesses of the Thirty made the previous government, that of the radical democrats, seem like pure gold. With the decrease in her naval power, Athens had no need to heed the *thetes*, and even when she regained it their voice was muted. Thus a moderate democracy was secured for many years.

Another city worthy of specific mention is Corcyra, for here the struggles between oligarchs and democrats and the resultant civil wars were particularly bloody. The spark which set the oligarchs and democrats at each other's throats came, as has been noted, from the neighbouring Corcyrean colony of Epidamnus. Shortly before the outbreak of the Peloponnesian War the Epidamnians expelled their aristocrats, who promptly joined with the neighbouring barbarians to attack Epidamnus. The democrats at Epidamnus requested aid from Corcyra, but were refused. They then turned to Corinth, which, although oligarchic, was nevertheless willing to aid the democrats of Epidamnus in order to strike against Corcyra. Corinth's support of Epidamnus led to war with Corcyra, which in turn helped to trigger the Peloponnesian War.

In 428 BC the Athenians induced certain Corcyreans to attempt to reaffirm their city's alliance with them. This act led to civil war. The oligarchs brought a charge against Peithias, a Corcyrean who had acted as Athens' representative, of trying to make Corcyra subject to Athens' domination. When the suit failed, Peithias brought his own suit against five of the wealthiest oligarchs for sacrilege. Since the democrats were in a majority, they convicted these oligarchs and levied an exorbitant fine. Unable to pay, these men led the oligarchs into the council meeting, and murdered Peithias and sixty other senators. Once in control they pledged a neutral policy in the Peloponnesian War. Civil war continued, however, and with the aid of the slaves in the city the democrats counter-attacked and won. At the approach of an Athenian fleet the democrats felt secure, and began to kill their oligarchic enemies. Fifty oligarchs who were taking refuge in the Temple of Hera were persuaded to surrender and promised a fair trial, but the trial proved a sham and they were swiftly executed. In the slaughter, Thucydides tells us, 'father slew son, men were dragged from the temples and slain near them, and some were walled up in the Temple of Dionysus and perished there. To such excess of savagery did the revolution go.'

The surviving oligarchs took refuge on Mount Istone, but when the Corcyrean democrats joined with the Athenian forces they reluctantly realized that the choice was death or surrender. Terrified of falling into the clutches of the democrats, they negotiated with the Athenians to surrender to them alone, on condition that they be tried at Athens. But the Corcyrean democrats wanted blood, and induced a few of the prisoners to attempt an escape. This action violated the terms of the surrender, and the Corcyreans were able to take custody of the prisoners. Sixty of them were dragged out of prison to run a gauntlet, and stabbed and beaten on their way. When these sixty were dead, the mob attacked the prison, and poured down arrows and tiles from the roof. A gruesome scene followed: some oligarchs tried to defend

148

themselves; others commited suicide by plunging arrows into their throats or strangling themselves. At daybreak, the Corcyreans, sated with slaughter, loaded the bodies on wagons, and hauled them out of the city. There was now scarcely an oligarch left alive in the city – an effective way to end the civil war.

Seventeen years later, in 410 BC, the tide of the Peloponnesian War was turning against Athens. The size of the oligarchic party in Corcyra had by then sufficiently increased to be once more a potent political force. Their number had been swelled by returning exiles, particularly those who had escaped the carnage of 428 BC. The oligarchs, who favoured the Spartans, planned to betray the city to them. To prevent this the democrats sent for an Athenian army, and with the aid of six hundred Athenian troops arrested and slew many oligarchs and drove more than a thousand into exile. They also freed those slaves and gave citizenship to those foreigners who had aided them against the oligarchs. After a few days some oligarchs who remained in the city seized the market-place and called back the exiles. Bloody fighting ensued, in which the oligarchs barely managed to get the upper hand, and, under their leadership, Corcyra reverted to her pre-war policy of neutrality. Diodorus Siculus remarks of this second civil war: 'Never in any state have there taken place such murders of citizens nor have there been greater quarrelling and contentiousness which culminated in bloodshed.' The oligarchic-democratic clash at Corcyra was essentially a class struggle, but because of the Peloponnesian War it tended to become an international political one. Like Athens, Corcyra was a naval power and thus depended on her lower classes to man her fleet. As in Athens, the democrats had the greatest popular support. This meant that even at the height of their power in 410 BC the oligarchs were able only to follow a policy of neutrality.

In the oligarchic-democratic struggles of the fifth century, as has been noted above, ideological loyalties superseded state ones. Recognizing this the Spartan general Brasidas said to the citizens of Acanthus: 'I have not come to join a faction, nor do I think that the freedom I am offering would be a real one if, regardless of your ancestral institutions, I should enslave the majority to the few or the minority to the multitude. That would be more galling than foreign rule.' In part, the willingness to betray a city to a foreign enemy is explained by the method of rule which the conquering enemy adopted. Usually he would leave the city more or less autonomous, possibly garrisoned, but in the hands of those who had betrayed the city. Thus when the democrats at Selymbria and Byzantium betrayed their cities to Alcibiades and Athens in 409/408 BC, Alcibiades installed a democratic government under the betrayers.

To drive Hippias from Athens in 510 BC the Alcmaeonids enlisted Spartan aid, knowing that after the expulsion they would be left in control. Similarly, when Isagoras was battling with Cleisthenes for supremacy in Athens in 508/507, he turned to Sparta for aid. He preferred Athens to be an oligarchy under Spartan domination than a free democracy. Plutarch records that on the eve of the battle of Plataea in 479, when Athens and Greece were fighting for their freedom against Persia, certain Athenians formed a conspiracy to overthrow the democracy and betray the state to Persia. The masterminds of the plot were members of families once rich and influential which had lost wealth and power with the growth of the democracy. Fortunately for Athens, Aristides discovered the plot and suppressed it. In 457 BC, just before the battle of Tanagra, some Athenian oligarchs secretly asked the Spartans to march on Athens and dissolve the democracy. The Athenians forestalled the plot by marching out to meet the Spartans. This treason was the work of an oligarchic club, or perhaps a combination of clubs. The democrats at Athens constantly feared a betrayal of their city to Sparta. When the herms were mutilated in 415 BC, the democrats immediately assumed that this was part of an oligarchic plot against the democracy.

During the oligarchic revolution of 411 the extreme wing of the oligarchs was preparing to betray Athens to Sparta. Thucydides observes: 'The charge was not a mere calumny, but had some foundation in the disposition of the ruling party. For what would have best pleased them would have been retaining the oligarchy in any case, to have preserved the Athenian empire over the allies; failing this, to keep merely their ships and walls, and to be independent; if this too proved impracticable, at any rate they would not see democracy restored, and themselves fall the first victims, but would rather bring in the enemy and come to terms with them, not caring if thereby the city lost walls and ships and everything else, provided that they could save their lives' (tr. B. Jowett). The Thirty gained control of Athens in 404 BC with the help of Lysander and the Spartans. They requested and obtained a Spartan military commander and seven hundred hoplites, and later requested more aid.

Examples of betrayals by oligarchs or democrats abound. About 492 BC the democrats at Aegina plotted to betray the island to the

Athenians, but they were discovered and seven hundred of them were massacred. The Peloponnesian War began with a betrayal. During the course of the war there were at least twenty-seven betrayals or attempted betrayals of cities. The oligarchs at Plataea in 431 BC opened the gates to the Thebans. Once in control, however, the Theban troops failed to crush their opponents and were beaten the next day. In his campaign in the north-west Aegean in the late 420s the Spartan general Brasidas took many cities, among them Torone and Mende, through the treason of oligarchs. It became the normal practice for an army faced with a city which refused to surrender to persuade the democrats or oligarchs inside the city to open the gates.

In the oligarchic-democratic struggles in Athens and elsewhere the courts became a frequent battlefield in which to attack opponents. Because of the nature of Athenian legal procedure the outcome of the trial often depended on the popularity of the accused. A fourth-century example shows the extent to which the courts could be used for political fights. Demosthenes was, for a time, arraigned every single day by his enemies on one accusation or another. In 462 BC, in his attack on the Areopagus, the old aristocratic council which remained as the last vestige of aristocratic administrative strength in Athens, Ephialtes made use of the courts; he prosecuted prominent members of the Areopagus, possibly before the *heliaea,* the popular court of appeals, to prevent their opposition to his reforms. Pericles was tried and convicted of bribery in 430 BC, probably through the efforts of the oligarchic faction and the radical democrats. In 406 BC political opponents managed to convict and execute the generals who had been in command at the battle of Arginusae, ostensibly because of their failure to rescue the shipwrecked survivors. The Thirty Tyrants condemned the democratic leader Cleophon to death on a trumped-up charge.

Another avenue of attack was the obstruction of legislation. This was usually accomplished by means of an indictment for proposing illegal measures, which would slow up and could even kill legislation. Other devices were used, such as caucuses of the oligarchic clubs, which voted *en bloc* in the assembly. Canvassing and bribery in assemblies was common. Harassing and interfering with speeches through interruptions, applause or jeering was another tactic. The oligarchic clubs were often the instigators of these devices. They also played an important role in elections.

Ostracism and assassination were other weapons of the political parties. We see both of these used in the democratic-oligarchic struggle in Athens over the powers of the Areopagus in 462/461 BC. We have no detailed information as to these powers; we only know that the Areopagus had some control over officials and laws, and sat as a court of first instance in some cases, for example, murder and impiety, and in others as the court of appeal. It was composed of ex-archons who served for a life term. Since the archons came from the top two classes, this meant that the Areopagus was an upper-class body. In 487 BC election to the archonship was changed from direct election to selection by lot. Thus, instead of being a chosen group of archons, elected by all segments of the populace, the Areopagus came to represent a cross-section of the aristocracy. The conservative oligarchic faction, led by Cimon, the son of Miltiades, opposed any change in the body. The democrats wished to eliminate the powers of the Areopagus as being an infringement of the sovereignty of the people: while other officers served for a single year, members of the Areopagus held their posts, as we have seen, for life, which gave it continuity and enhanced power.

In 462 Cimon persuaded the Athenians to send troops under his command to aid Sparta in her war against her helots, then in revolt. In his absence the democratic leader Ephialtes successfully proposed laws transferring some of the judicial power of the Areopagus to the *heliaea*, and others of its functions to the Council of Five Hundred. Meanwhile Cimon arrived with his Athenian troops to help Sparta, but his aid was refused. He returned in disgrace to Athens and was ostracized soon afterwards. The oligarchs, without a leader, sought revenge, and assassinated Ephialtes. The Areopagus, the last constitutional stronghold of the aristocrats and oligarchs, was relegated to non-political functions. From this point on the aristocrats could rule only with the sufferance of the people.

The fact that ostracism could be applied only once a year, and that it entailed complicated legal procedures and canvassing, made it only partially effective as a weapon in the oligarchic-democratic struggle. Details of most of the ostracisms in Athens are lacking, but it was used by both factions. The first ostracism was that of Hipparchus in 487 BC: most probably he was oligarchic in sympathy. During the wranglings of the 480s and 470s Themistocles and Aristides were ostracized. The most severe clash of oligarchs and democrats over ostracism, besides Cimon's case, occurred in 444 BC, when a crisis between the democrats, led by Pericles, and the oligarchs, led by Thucydides, the son of Melesias, resulted in the ostracism of Thucydides. In 418/417 BC, in the midst of a struggle between the existing political factions, Hyperbolus, the democratic leader, attempted to secure the ostracism of Alcibiades. Counteracting this attempt, Alcibiades joined his faction to two others, those of Nicias and Phaeax, both of various oligarchic hues, and thus effected Hyperbolus' own ostracism. This was the last use of ostracism at Athens. Plutarch complains that no worthless or disreputable person had ever been ostracized before Hyperbolus, and it was this which killed the institution. The real reason for its demise, however, seems to have been that there were more efficient ways of disposing of opponents.

Assassination was much more common a device than ostracism in dealing with political enemies since it was so much easier to carry out. It was practised more frequently by oligarchs and oligarchic clubs than by the democrats. The Athenian democratic leader Hyperbolus, for example, was assassinated by oligarchs at Samos in 411 BC. To take control of Athens in 411 the oligarchs first murdered the democratic leader Androcles, and then anyone else in the assembly and council who objected to the oligarchic *coup*. The Thirty at Athens killed over fifteen hundred people, some by assassination, some by judicial murder. The democrats at Athens managed only one important assassination at the end of the fifth century, that of the oligarchic leader Phrynichus. Elsewhere, however, as at Corcyra, both sides resorted frequently to assassination in this period.

Despite their political reconciliation in 403 BC, resentment and hostility between oligarchs and democrats at Athens persisted in the first few years of the fourth century. The year 399 saw the trial of two oligarchs, Socrates and Andocides, both for impiety. Socrates, probably not guilty, was condemned, while Andocides, probably guilty, was acquitted. The execution of Socrates has been viewed as an example of the dangers of mass rule, the folly of democracy, and an anti-intellectual, anti-individualist act. For Hegel, Socrates' greatness and the force of his ideas made his trial inevitable. Plato regarded him as a martyr, and indeed he has become one in Western tradition because of his and Plato's importance in the history of philosophy. In reality, his martyrdom was self-imposed, almost a suicide.

Socrates was born about 470 BC. Like his father he was trained as a stone-cutter. He married a woman called Xanthippe and had three sons by her. A confirmed urban dweller and devoted to Athens, he served as a hoplite in several battles during the Peloponnesian War. In 406 BC he was president of the assembly on the day the Athenian generals were tried for their failure to rescue their shipwrecked men after the battle of Arginusae. He opposed their being tried *en masse* as being illegal, and unsuccessfully pressed for individual trials. He was a member of the Three Thousand citizens who had been created by the Thirty, and was a close friend and teacher of Critias, Plato's second cousin and the leader of the Thirty, as well as of Plato's uncle, Charmides, another member of the Thirty. Nevertheless, he refused to arrest a certain Leon of Salamis when ordered to do so by the Thirty. In 399 BC, under the restored democrats, he was tried for impiety and 'corrupting the youth', found guilty, condemned to death and executed.

Socrates left no written works, but through the influence which he exerted on his pupil Plato, he became one of the most important figures in Western philosophy. Because of his position and the myth which was created first by Plato and then perpetuated by later generations, much about his teachings and trial has been obscured.

Socrates was regarded by the Athenians as the most eminent of the sophists, a group of philosophers, often itinerant, who became prominent in the mid-fifth century and later. To the people of Athens Socrates was a symbol of the free thinking which in the late fifth century had caused crisis on all levels, in religion, ethics, morals and politics. The Ionian philosophers, beginning with Thales in the early sixth century, had speculated about the origin and nature of the universe. In the mid-fifth century a reaction set in, led by Zeno of Elea whose astute analyses of space, motion and time encouraged scepticism about all cosmology and ontology. The most important philosophical problems concerned not cosmology, but epistemology and ethics. This new trend is seen in the words of Protagoras: 'man is the measure of all things; of the being of things that are and of the non-being of things that are not.' From this the sophists formed the corollary that there were two arguments, the weaker and the stronger. Relativism allowed the weaker argument to become stronger, if supported by a convincing exponent. Thus the sophists began to train their pupils in rhetoric, the art of persuasion.

The rationalistic trends of the sophists spread to medicine, particularly to the teachings of Hippocrates of Cos. He revolutionized medicine by maintaining that diseases are due only to natural causes. He says of epilepsy, for example: 'With regard to the so-called "sacred disease" it appears to me to be in no respect more divine or sacred than other diseases, but to have a natural origin like other complaints. . . .

90, 91 Impiety charges were commonly employed against political enemies in Athens. Left, Aspasia, Pericles' intellectual Milesian mistress, suffered at the hands of her lover's opponents. Right, Socrates, 'the gadfly of the Athenians', who came to embody for many of his fellow citizens the demoralizing new ideas apparently responsible for their misfortunes.

They [doctors] use the divinity as a cloak and screen to cover their own inability to benefit the patient and to hide their ignorance, and consider this affliction "sacred".'

    The relativism and rationalism of the sophists had its most serious effect in undermining the traditional religion of the Greeks. It was this attack on religion, the 'new morality' and dangerous ideas of people like Euripides and Socrates, that antagonized the populace of Athens. Socrates' trial is often viewed as an anti-intellectual act directed at a gadfly who was trying to bring truth and enlightenment to Athens. But, although hostility to his intellectual teachings probably contributed to the guilty verdict against Socrates, basically his trial was motivated by his political actions and political teachings. Throughout the fourth century it was generally held that Socrates was executed for being the teacher of Critias and Alcibiades, the charge against which Xenophon primarily feels it necessary to defend him.

Socrates was an oligarch both by inclination and by political alignment. His very philosophy was anti-democratic. He believed that the expert should manage affairs: the expert in shipbuilding should build ships, the expert teacher should teach the young. By the same token the state should be ruled by experts in statecraft, not by the masses who have no specialized talents. Socrates therefore opposed the election of officials by lot, a procedure which was considered highly democratic. He taught these anti-democratic ideas to his pupils, most of whom were aristocrats, almost anti-democratic by birth, and who in practice turned out to be enemies of the democracy, such as Critias, or traitors to Athens herself, such as Alcibiades and later Xenophon. While the desire to have experts in statesmanship govern may have been an oligarchic tendency in Socrates, given the rather primitive Greek idea of democracy, the same desire in Thomas Jefferson (an 'aristocracy of virtue and talents', a 'natural aristocracy') was democratic. The method of choosing the experts and of holding them accountable is the issue. Jefferson expected them to be elected by the citizenry, and, if they failed, deposed by the citizenry. Although Jefferson agreed with Socrates (and Plato) that rule by lot was patently absurd, he loathed Plato's ideal state and the *Republic*, which he had read carefully and repeatedly.

The inclusion of Socrates among the Three Thousand full citizens appointed by the Thirty Tyrants shows that in fact as well as in word he was an oligarch. In his defence speech as presented by Plato in his *Apology* Socrates very carefully points out that when the Thirty ordered him to arrest Leon of Salamis he had refused to comply, although this failure to obey orders imperilled his life. But the very fact that the test was enjoined upon Socrates shows his close connections with the Thirty, who made it a practice to bind their allies to them through a common crime. For example, thirty metics were chosen to be arrested, one by each of the Thirty. When Eratosthenes, one of the Thirty, opposed the arrest of Lysias and his brother, the Thirty forced him to make the arrest personally. For the same purpose the Thirty coerced the Three Thousand citizens into condemning the inhabitants of Eleusis to death. By their orders for the arrest of Leon, the Thirty were apparently trying to ensure Socrates' allegiance to them. The fact that Socrates refused only indicates that he was not one of the extreme oligarchs.

In 399 BC both Athens and the restored democrats were making great strides in solidifying their position. Antyus, Archinus and Thrasybulus had worked hard to reconcile the Three Thousand to the rest of the population, particularly by their vigorous defence of the amnesty of 403 BC. It was only through the unstable political conditions in Sparta, arising from the antagonism between Lysander and the Spartan kings, that Athens was able to maintain her tenuous freedom and the democracy. Socrates, however, with his disturbing teachings, was a source of irritation. Thus Anytus resolved to silence him and thereby eliminate one more threat both to the political security of the state and to the reconciliation between oligarchy and democracy.

Anytus was faced with the problem of doing this without violating the amnesty of 403 BC, which he was scrupulous in observing. Isocrates praises him for not trying to regain his vast holdings which had been confiscated by the Thirty – they were now in the hands of new owners and could not be touched within the provisions of the amnesty. Further, although Anytus was a political opponent of Andocides, he came to his aid when he was among those tried for the mutilation of the herms and the profanation of the Eleusinian Mysteries on the eve of the Sicilian Expedition. Anytus probably followed this course in the belief that Andocides was protected by the amnesty. Since Anytus could not in all conscience prosecute Socrates for events that occurred before 403 BC, he needed fresh grounds on which to try him. It must be emphasized that Anytus was not trying to have Socrates killed; his purpose was to silence him and he hoped to do this by forcing him into exile. If ostracism had still been practised in 399, Anytus would almost certainly have used this as his weapon. Since he could not, he sought to try him on the vague charges of impiety and immorality. The indictment was sworn to by Meletus, and charged that Socrates was 'guilty of not believing in the gods in which the city believes, and of introducing other new divinities. He is also guilty of corrupting the youth. The penalty proposed is death.' Since the penalty for impiety was not fixed, the prosecutor usually proposed as severe a penalty as possible. The defendant was left to propose an acceptable counter-penalty, and the jury would then decide the sentence. The counter-proposal Socrates would be expected to make, if convicted, was exile. Instead he said he thought himself worthy of the highest honour granted by the state, maintenance for life at public expense in the Prytaneum, and he finally proposed a trivial fine which, he told the court, would be paid for him by his friends. The jury of

501 members had voted 281 to 220 for conviction. After Socrates' frivolous counter-proposal the jury voted for the death penalty, this time by a margin of 361 to 140.

After his conviction there was a delay of several weeks in carrying out the sentence because of an Athenian sacred embassy to Delos, during which no executions were permitted. According to Plato, Socrates was not closely guarded and was given every opportunity to escape. His friends urged this course, but he staunchly refused, maintaining that death was preferable to exile from his tribe and city. He then drank the hemlock and died, uncompromising and uncompromised.

Two charges were used in fifth-century Athens to attack an enemy, bribery and impiety. They were used in much the same way as the United States government has used the charge of conspiracy. The philosopher Anaxagoras may have been tried for impiety as part of a political attack on Pericles. Aspasia, Pericles' mistress, is said to have been charged with impiety and prostitution, though these stories may be fictitious. Socrates was specifically charged with disbelieving in the city's gods and introducing new ones. Yet he is presented both by Plato and by Xenophon as a man of deep piety who customarily observed the rites and sacrifices for the gods. Besides, if the introduction of new gods into Athens was a crime, many an Athenian was guilty. The introduction of Asclepius, a Greek god, was an act of state, but the cults of numerous foreign gods, Phrygian Cybele, Thracian Bendis and others, had already gained adherents in Athens. Worship of many of these was sooner or later permitted or encouraged by decree of the state. Socrates was not accused of practising foreign rites, but of believing in his inner voice, his *daimonion*, which acted as his conscience. Given the religious temperament of Athens, this was surely a flimsy basis for prosecution.

As for the charge of 'corrupting the youth', Socrates probably had homosexual affairs with some of his pupils, but the Greeks seldom prosecuted for acts of this sort, except to harass. Intellectual corruption was not a crime in Athens, and thus, whatever the prosecutor meant by 'corrupting the youth', it was at most secondary to the main charge of impiety.

In the Greek legal system questions of fact and law were not clearly distinguished. The jury decided both matters – whether a law had been violated and whether the accused had committed the act – and usually treated them as a single issue. Thus someone could be charged

92 The Anatolian mother-goddess Cybele, whose cult, involving exotic ritual and ecstatic states, seems to have reached Greece in the fifth century BC.

under a law without there having been a clear violation of that law. This was particularly true with regard to impiety, especially where no single sacrilegious act had been committed. In the case of Socrates it was therefore up to the jury to decide whether those acts of which he was accused constituted impiety. Those acts which other Athenians were daily committing were deemed criminally impious only when committed by him. Socrates had been active for many decades in Athens and had been publicly attacked and ridiculed most actively by the comic playwright Aristophanes (in the *Clouds*) in the late 420s. Whatever animosity and hatred existed towards Socrates, it was never sufficient to prompt people to remove him by legal means until 399 BC. At that juncture his oligarchic sympathies and teachings were regarded as a threat to the democracy, and another life was claimed by the oligarchic-democratic conflict.

The clashes of the fifth century in Athens were elements in a class struggle at the end of which the middle and lower classes emerged dominant. Cleisthenes had allied himself to the *demos* in order to gain political power, and he had then set out to break the power of the old aristocratic clans by his tribal and constitutional reforms. At that time two factions arose, the democrats, the poorer classes of society, and the oligarchs, a coalition of the wealthier class and the old aristocrats. Aristocrats remained able to dominate the state because they led both factions. As we noted, during the Persian War and subsequently when Athens was becoming a major sea power and the master of the Delian League, the *thetes* made a greater military contribution to the state and concomitantly attained greater rights in government. They were democrats and their military importance strengthened the democratic faction, which previous to this had been dominated by the hoplites. A crisis in the struggle came in 462 BC over the power of the Areopagus, with the democrats emerging victorious. Within a few years the democrats further broadened the base of government when, in 457/456 BC, the *zeugitai* were allowed to hold the archonship. About this time an innovation was introduced by Pericles, pay for jurors and state service. Before this state service had entailed financial hardship, since the demands of office forced the participant temporarily to forego his regular employment. Since *zeugitai* or *thetes* who were barely making ends meet would not sacrifice their livelihood to serve on a jury, the wealthier elements of the population tended to run the state. With the introduction of pay, however, even if inadequate to live on, the poorer elements of the population could now afford to participate in the rule of the state.

The struggles and faction fights between oligarchs and democrats continued in Athens, with the democrats overwhelmingly holding the upper hand under Pericles until his death in 429 BC. With the death of Pericles a change occurred in the method of government. The lower classes began to take direct control of the assembly and discovered that through this body they could rule the state. Until 429 the means to power lay in being a *strategos* or general of one's tribe. In many states, especially democracies like Athens, there was a fear that the chief official would use his office as a means of establishing a tyranny. To safeguard against this the office tenure of the chief official was usually limited to a single term of a year, and where the office could be held again, a long interval between terms was required. Military matters, however, had to be in the hands of the most competent, and therefore in Athens a yearly re-election was not only permitted, but even common. Popular control of the assembly, used by the Athenian demagogues such as Cleon, proved a doubly effective means to power: it did not necessitate yearly election and avoided the risk of punishment for failure of policies. A general could be fined or executed on some trumped-up charge if his policy was faring badly but a demagogue in the assembly could not legally be touched if the policies which he advocated fared ill. Further, the people could now exercise direct control over policy instead of the indirect control which they had exercised through elected officials. The weakness of this system, of course, was that specific policy could too easily be affected by demagogy. At this time the democrats began to discard their aristocratic leaders.

Tensions within the polis were generated by changing economic, military and social conditions, which undermined the unity that had been based on common religion, history, customs, language and kinship. The introduction of trade and colonization in the late ninth and eighth centuries disrupted the static agrarian society, as did the emergence of hoplite warfare in the late eighth or early seventh century. The non-aristocratic elements, consisting of the new rich and the hoplites, often with the aid of tyrants, battled for control of the state in the seventh and sixth centuries. By the sixth and fifth centuries the conflict within the polis had polarized into oligarchs against democrats. In cities such as Athens, as the lower classes tried to move from participation in government under the leadership of aristocrats to control of the state, the polis was racked by betrayals, treasons, judicial wranglings, ostracisms, assassinations and civil wars.

VI EPILOGUE AND CONCLUSIONS

The restrictive citizenship practices of the Greek polis, reflected in internal dissension, fragmentation through colonization and the inability to absorb and integrate conquests, were a fundamental factor in its disunity. These practices were sustained, and to a certain extent caused by the tribal and kinship system and class strife. In the first instance, since the polis was in many ways a sophisticated tribal organization, citizens of one state had no clan or kinship position in another state. Because of the common feelings of 'Greekness', however, a citizen of one polis might live in another polis as a resident alien. The development of the polis in the ninth and eighth centuries served to attenuate tribal loyalties between regions and to strengthen the importance of the clans, the phratries and the tribes within the city. As the strength of the kinship system deteriorated, restrictive citizenship practices relaxed to some extent. We have seen that Athens was the most progressive of the Greek states in liberalizing her citizenship practices. This started with the reforms of Cleisthenes at the end of the sixth century, which replaced the four kinship tribes as the basis of political administration with ten artificially created tribes, based on locality. Admission to one of the ten tribes thus became psychologically less difficult than to one of the four tribes, since there were no kinship ties in the former. Not until nearly two centuries after Cleisthenes, however, did the barriers to foreign residents at Athens give way, although class strife had largely been resolved by the fourth century.

The attitudes which fostered restrictive citizenship practices were further undermined by the intellectual revolution at the end of the fifth century and the beginning of the fourth, and by the leaders of that revolution, the sophists and their followers, as well as by many who advocated Greek unity. In the fourth century numerous Greeks favoured unification in theory and attempted it in practice. The principle of autonomy of the polis still survived, but it gradually began to be discarded in all but name. Despite the conservatism of his political theory, Plato, who hearkened back to an ideal polis, recognized that Greek states constituted a common society. Isocrates, the great exponent of Panhellenism, exhorted Greeks to find unity less

163

in blood than in a common education and common type of mind, and then to unite against the common enemy, Persia. Strides were made towards unity in the fourth century in some locales by monarchies, such as that of Dionysius I of Syracuse, and ultimately in the last forty years of the century unity was achieved by the monarchy of Macedon under Philip, Alexander, and their political heirs.

With the general breakdown of the polis in the early fourth century and the loss of confidence in it as a viable institution, the federated leagues emerged as the dominant powers in Greece. Generally they proved strong at a time when the world was being changed beyond recognition by Alexander and the Hellenistic monarchies which followed him. Consequently they remained too small for success on any but a local level.

Federal states developed from tribal units or groups, such as the Boeotians, Achaeans, Aetolians or Arcadians. Among these groups the feelings of tribal kinship, which might include a tradition of co-operation in war or in a special religious cult, tended to override narrow clan or kinship relations. Since these tribal areas were much slower to urbanize than the regions where the major cities had sprung up, feelings of tribal kinship continued to dominate them even after they had developed commercial and political centres. Consequently a tribal league had few inhibitions in granting citizenship to all members of its own tribal area.

In its structure the federal league resembled a huge polis. Its different components often had common laws, common weights and measures, common coins and common magistrates. Unlike the polis, however, it had no single central fortification for all its inhabitants and it was more liberal in its citizenship practices. League citizenship existed simultaneously with local citizenship in smaller communities which might be either tribes or small city states. Citizens fell under the jurisdiction of both federal and local authorities. The rights of local citizenship, voting and holding office could only be exercised in one's native city. Political rights in the federal states were exercised through voting in a city for representatives to the league. This development mirrored the way in which members of a polis voted by tribe for representatives to govern the city. In the normal federal state citizens could own land in all the cities of the confederacy. Paralleling the institutions of the polis, most federal leagues had a council (*boule*) and assembly (*ecclesia*). The federal assemblies met, however, much less frequently than the polis assembly, for example twice a year in the

Aetolian League and four times in the Achaean, as compared with at least forty meetings a year of the assembly at Athens. Boeotia, however, had only a *boule*, and thus enjoyed outright representative government. The army was composed of contingents from various cities, and an individual served with the regiment of the polis of which he was a resident, rather than that of which he was a citizen. A confederacy required a capital for the transaction of its business, usually located in the strongest centre of the league, such as Thebes in Boeotia or Megalopolis in Arcadia.

Unlike the polis, which was administered by the council and assembly, the federal league had as its head either a general or, at times, a cabinet. In the case of the Boeotian confederacy, the first such league to become a major power in Greece in the fifth century, a board of Boeotarchs consisting of a general and a board of magistrates ruled. The Achaean League followed the more usual form of a general (at times two generals) with an advisory body drawn from the League members. Thus federal leagues adopted many of the institutions of the polis, but not its rigidity.

The federal leagues were markedly different from the great Peloponnesian and Delian Leagues of the fifth century. The latter were symmachies, that is, permanent loose alliances of independent city states where no shared citizenship existed, nor could individuals own land in any but their own polis. In symmachies the executive department was in the hands of the state which exercised hegemony and provided any administrative officials required, Sparta in the Peloponnesian League and Athens in the Delian and Second Athenian Leagues.

To create federal states of any importance it was necessary to cross ethnic boundaries and admit members of other tribes. This is perhaps best seen in the Achaean League, probably the most important of the Greek federal states. In its early stages at the beginning of the fourth century BC it admitted non-Achaeans to citizenship. According to Polybius, Achaea changed from a united kingdom to a republican federal state. Some time before 389 BC federal citizenship was instituted when Achaea acquired Calydon and made the Calydonians Achaean citizens. The Achaeans also held Naupactus and incorporated her citizens into Achaean citizenship. The Achaean League, dissolved in the early third century, was revived in 281/280 BC. From 280 to 255 the member cities elected a federal secretary and two generals on a rotation system, with the city whose turn it was to furnish the chief official in command. Under Aratus the Achaean League became a

165

major power in the Peloponnese and in Greece, emerging as the leading member of the Hellenistic League organized by Antigonus Doson in 224/223 BC. When the Romans became involved in Greece in 198 BC the Achaeans aligned themselves with them. The Achaean League united and merged the peoples of the Peloponnese into one nation. Achaea became the name of the Peloponnese and also of the chief Roman province in Greece.

The federal leagues represented an efficient form of government and they might have been able to bring some unity to Greece; but they failed because their emergence was ill-timed. The very factor which allowed the federal leagues to develop as strong powers, the breakdown of the polis, also allowed the formation of a new world order under Alexander. By the time the federal leagues emerged it was too late for them to have any real impact on Greece. Had the Achaean League existed in the fifth century, it might have been able to unite much of Greece; but the political and social institutions of that era precluded its existence as a potent force.

The Greek polis failed politically. Its particularism prevented unity, encouraged warfare within the state and among states and ultimately contributed to the subjection of Greece by the Macedonian kings. The polis system was a reflection of Greek character, of its individualism, independence and self-absorption; at the same time it reinforced those very tendencies.

Disunity was, as we have seen, a salient feature of the Greek city state. Unity is not, however, necessarily the ideal. It usually brings with it internal harmony and peace, but not necessarily survival, strength or vitality. When Persia under Xerxes attacked Greece in the early fifth century she was a united empire, yet she was defeated by an uneasy coalition of usually disunited Greek city states. The united Egyptian empire, on the other hand, was easily defeated by the Persians. A Utopian united Greece might have produced a peaceful existence, but the vitality of the polis might have been lost. Alexander brought a certain unity to the world by conquest, as did Rome through her vast and long-enduring empire, but the creativity of both empires did not compare to that of the small Greek state. The sixth and fifth centuries in Greece represent one of the most vital and innovatory eras in history. Science and mathematics, though not invented by the Greeks, were given their modern bases in this period. Ionian philosophers such as Thales began mathematical studies which reached peaks in the fifth century under Pythagoras and later in the third century under Euclid. Atomic theory was developed in Abdera. Hippocrates, the father of Western medicine, sprang from the polis society, and his works, along with Galen's of the second century AD, formed the basis of medicine until the last century. Many genres of literature were given their form, if not invented, by the Greeks of the polis – tragedy by Aeschylus, Sophocles and Euripides, comedy by Aristophanes, who was such a genius of political satire that even 2,400 years later the military junta in Greece has banned many of his plays because their barbs still smart. The science of history began with Herodotus and Thucydides. Socrates and Plato, citizens of the polis of Athens, laid the foundation of much of Western philosophy and political theory. Art, architecture and the great sculptures of Pheidias, Polycleitus, Praxiteles were all products of the polis. In short, much of Western culture owes its basis to the genius of the Greek polis. It is interesting to observe, in the light of fifth-century Athens, that the murderous politics described in Machiavelli's *The Prince* and elsewhere co-existed with Leonardo, Michelangelo and Raphael.

In the cultural and political unity which Alexander brought to most of the known world from Egypt to India by his conquests, the achievements of the polis were unmatched. Though under Alexander and his successors the cultivation of the arts was widespread, literature and science flourished and vast libraries proliferated, it was the culture of scholasticism, not of the seminal creativity of the polis.

The largest unit is not necessarily politically the best. An organization or state that grows large provides a measure of stability for its people. But in order to function it must, as the Persian empire did, divide to create smaller administrative units; and with this a vast, often inefficient, bureaucracy arises. Unity and larger political systems escalate the levels of warfare. When little Croton annihilated neighbouring Sybaris in southern Italy at the end of the sixth century BC, the Milesians in Asia Minor, who enjoyed extensive trade with Sybaris, shed tears. But, when Athens went to war with Sparta, two great power blocs clashed: instead of a conflict between two small states, half of the Greek world ranged itself against the other half. The polis failed in the sense that it could not produce a stable political system in the face of economic and social changes. However, the very factors which caused this failure made the polis a centre for intellectual and cultural productivity and for a creative genius which might otherwise never have matured.

CHRONOLOGY

BC

early 8th century	Greeks settle Al Mina in Syria as a trading centre.
c. 750 onwards	Greeks expand to the west; colonization in Italy and Sicily (*c.* 735).
late 8th century	Lelantine War between Chalcis and Eretria. Oriental influences begin in Greek art.
early 7th century	'Lycurgan Constitution' at Sparta.
c. 668–660	Sparta crushes Messenian revolt.
c. 650	Cypselus overthrows Bacchiad aristocracy at Corinth and makes himself tyrant. Tyrannies at Sicyon, Megara.
c. 630	Thera founds Cyrene.
625	Periander becomes tyrant at Corinth.
c. 620	Draco's law code at Athens.
594	Solon's reforms at Athens.
585	Death of Periander.
582	Tyranny at Corinth falls.
561	Peisistratus seizes the government at Athens.
546	Final establishment of Peisistratus' tyranny at Athens.
528/527	Hippias and Hipparchus succeed their father as tyrants at Athens.
514	Assassination of Hipparchus by Harmodius and Aristogeiton.
510	Hippias expelled from Athens by Spartans at the instigation of the Alcmaeonids. Struggle between Isagoras and Cleisthenes.
507	Cleisthenes' reforms at Athens.
507/506	Spartan intervention in Athens repulsed.
499	Revolt of Greek cities in Asia Minor from Persia. Athens sends assistance.
494	Persians suppress Greek revolt in Asia Minor.
490	Persians invade Greece. Athenians victorious at Marathon.
487	Ostracism first used at Athens.
483–480	Athenians build a large fleet to combat Persia.
480	Second Persian invasion of Greece under Xerxes. Battles of Thermopylae, Artemisium and Salamis.
479	Greeks victorious over Persians at Plataea and Mycale.
478	Formation of Delian League.
471	Unsuccessful attempt of Naxos to secede from the League.
470	Ostracism of Themistocles.
469	Victory of Delian League under Cimon over Persians at Eurymedon.

465	Unsuccessful revolt of Thasos from Delian League.
464	Messenian revolt at Sparta.
462/461	Reforms of Ephialtes at Athens. Ephialtes assassinated and Cimon exiled. Rise of Pericles.
460–445	First Peloponnesian War.
454	Treasury of Delian League moved from Delos to Athens.
451	Pericles' law restricting citizenship to children of two citizen parents.
449	Peace between Persia and Greeks.
446	Revolt of Boeotia and Megara from Athenian empire.
444	Athens founds Thurii.
440	Revolt of Samos from Athenian empire.
437	Athens founds Amphipolis.
431–404	Peloponnesian War.
429	Death of Pericles.
427–424	First expedition of Athens against Sicily.
424	Brasidas' expedition to Thrace. Thucydides exiled from Athens.
422	Battle of Amphipolis. Cleon and Brasidas killed.
421	Peace of Nicias, ending first part of Peloponnesian War.
420	Alcibiades' intrigues, leading to Athenian alliance with Argos.
418	Sparta defeats Argos and her allies at Mantinea. Athens not officially involved.
416	Melian population destroyed.
415	Athenian expedition to Sicily.
414	Sparta resumes active warfare against Athens.
413	Athenian armies and navy annihilated in Sicily.
411	Oligarchic revolution at Athens (the Four Hundred) and institution of moderate oligarchy (the Five Thousand).
410	Restoration of democracy at Athens.
406	Athenian victory at Arginusae over Spartan fleet; trial of Athenian generals.
405	Athenian fleet virtually destroyed at Aegospotami, effectively ending Athenian resistance to Sparta.
404	Athens surrenders; Thirty Tyrants gain control of the government.
403	Restoration of democracy and amnesty.
399	Socrates condemned and executed.
371	Thebes defeats Sparta at Leuctra.
362	Thebes defeats Sparta at Mantinea; the Theban leader Epaminondas killed.
338	Philip of Macedon defeats Athens and Thebes at Chaeronea.
336	Murder of Philip and accession of Alexander to the throne of Macedon.
334	Alexander and his armies cross into Asia.

SELECT BIBLIOGRAPHY

This bibliography is intended to guide the reader to the most important works on matters discussed in this book. It is by no means complete, and with a few exceptions works in languages other than English have been omitted, as have articles in journals.

GENERAL

The best one-volume histories of Greece are those of J. B. Bury, *A History of Greece*, ed. R. Meiggs (London 1951); and N. G. L. Hammond, *A History of Greece to 322 B.C.* (Oxford 1959). For 700–500 BC, A. R. Burn, *The Lyric Age of Greece* (London and New York 1960). For 800–400 BC, W. G. Forrest, *The Emergence of Greek Democracy* (London 1966). The *Cambridge Ancient History* (12 vols, Cambridge 1923–39), vols 3–5 offers a more comprehensive treatment. General short introductions are A. Andrewes, *The Greeks* (London 1967); H. D. F. Kitto, *The Greeks* (Harmondsworth 1951, Baltimore 1967).

CHAPTER I

Adkins, A. W. H., *Merit and Responsibility: A Study of Greek Values* (Oxford 1960).
Cary, M., *The Geographic Background of Greek and Roman History* (Oxford 1949).
Dodds, E. R., *The Greeks and the Irrational* (Berkeley and Los Angeles 1951).
Gardiner, E. N., *Greek Athletic Sports and Festivals* (London 1910).
Gouldner, A. W., *The Hellenic World* (New York 1969).
Heyden, A. A. M. van der, and Scullard, H. H., *Atlas of the Classical World* (London 1959).
Lacey, W. K., *The Family in Classical Greece* (London 1968).
Myres, J. L., *Geographical History in Greek Lands* (Oxford 1953).
Slater, P., *The Glory of Hera* (Boston 1968).

CHAPTER II

The best general treatment of the Greek polis is Victor Ehrenberg's *The Greek State* (London 1959). Old, but none the less brilliant and valuable, is Fustel de Coulanges's *La Cité Antique (The Ancient City)*, of which numerous translations are available in English. Of wider scope is Max Weber's *The City* (Glencoe, Ill., 1958, London 1960), and also Lewis Mumford's *The City in History* (London and New York 1961).

Barker, E., *Greek Political Theory* (London 1960).
Desborough, V. R. D'A., *The Last Mycenaeans and their Successors* (Oxford 1964).
Finley, M. I., *Early Greece: the Bronze and Archaic Ages* (London and New York 1970).
Glotz, G., *The Greek City* (London 1929).
Samuel, A. E., *The Mycenaeans in History* (Englewood Cliffs, N.J., 1966).
Sinclair, T. A., *History of Greek Political Thought* (London 1952).
Starr, C. G., *The Origins of Greek Civilization, 1100–650 B.C.* (New York 1961, London 1962).
Vermeule, E. T., *Greece in the Bronze Age* (London and Chicago 1964).
Wilamowitz-Moellendorff, U. von, *Aristotele und Athen* (Berlin 1966).

CHAPTER III

Boardman, J., *The Greeks Overseas* (Harmondsworth 1964).
Cook, J.M., *The Greeks in Ionia and the East* (London 1962).
Dunbabin, T.J., *The Greeks and their Eastern Neighbours* (London 1957).
——, *The Western Greeks* (Oxford 1948).
Finley, M.I., *A History of Sicily I: Ancient Sicily to the Arab Conquest* (London 1968).
Freeman, E.A., *The History of Sicily* (4 vols, Oxford 1891–94).
Graham, A.J., *Colony and Mother City in Ancient Greece* (Manchester 1964).

CHAPTER IV

Boer, W. den, *Laconian Studies* (Amsterdam 1954).
Bradeen, D.W., 'The Popularity of the Athenian Empire', *Historia*, 1960, 257–69.
Chrimes, K.M.T., *Ancient Sparta* (Manchester 1949).
Ferguson, W.S., *Greek Imperialism* (London and New York 1913).
Forrest, W.G., *A History of Sparta 950–192 B.C.* (London 1968).
Hignett, C., *A History of the Athenian Constitution* (Oxford 1967).
Huxley, G.L., *Early Sparta* (London 1962).
Jones, A.H.M., *Athenian Democracy* (Oxford 1957).
——, *Sparta* (Oxford 1967).
Michell, H., *Sparta* (Cambridge 1952).
Romilly, J. de, *Thucydides and Athenian Imperialism*, tr. P. Thody (New York 1958, Oxford 1963).
Ste Croix, G.E.M. de, 'The Character of the Athenian Empire', *Historia*, 1954, 257–69.

CHAPTER V

Adcock, F.E., *The Greek and Macedonian Art of War* (Berkeley and Los Angeles 1957).
Andrewes, A., *The Greek Tyrants* (London 1956).
Burn, A.R., *Persia and the Greeks* (London and New York 1962).
——, *The World of Hesiod* (London 1936, New York 1966).
Calhoun, G.M., *Athenian Clubs in Politics and Litigation* (Austin 1913).
Chroust, A.H., *Socrates, Man and Myth* (London and Notre Dame, Ind., 1957).
Clerc, M., *Les Métèques Atheniens* (Paris 1893).
Ehrenberg, V., *From Solon to Socrates* (London 1968).
Eliot, C.W.J., *The Coastal Demes of Attica* (Toronto 1962).
Finley, M.I. (ed.), *Slavery in Classical Antiquity* (Cambridge 1960).
Finley, M.I., *Studies in Land and Credit in Ancient Athens 500–200 B.C.* (New Brunswick, N.J., 1951).
——, *The World of Odysseus* (London 1956, New York 1965).
Freeman, K., *The Work and Life of Solon* (London 1926).
French, A., *The Growth of the Athenian Economy* (London and New York 1964).
Gigon, O., *Sokrates* (Bern 1947).
Glotz, G., *Ancient Greece at Work* (London and New York 1926).
Gomme, A.W., *The Population of Athens in the Fifth and Fourth Centuries B.C.* (Oxford 1933).
Haarhoff, T.J., *The Stranger at the Gate* (Oxford 1948).

Hasebroek, J., *Trade and Politics in Ancient Greece* (London 1933).
Heichelheim, F. M., *An Ancient Economic History* (3 vols, Leiden 1958–70).
Kraay, C. M., and Hirmer, M., *Greek Coins* (London 1966).
Lorimer, H.L., 'The Hoplite Phalanx', *Annual of the British School at Athens*, 1947, 76–138.
Losada, L. A., *The Fifth Column in the Peloponnesian War* (Leiden 1972).
Michell, H., *The Economics of Ancient Greece* (Cambridge 1957).
Pritchett, W. K., *The Five Attic Tribes after Cleisthenes* (Baltimore 1943).
Snodgrass, A., *Early Greek Armour and Weapons* (Edinburgh 1964).
——, 'The Hoplite Reform and History', *Journal of Hellenic Studies*, 1965, 110–22.
Ure, P. N., *The Origin of Tyranny* (Cambridge 1922, New York 1962).
Westermann, W.L., *The Slave Systems of Greek and Roman Antiquity* (Philadelphia 1955).
Woodhouse, W.J., *Solon the Liberator* (London 1938, New York 1965).

CHAPTER VI
Griffith, G. T., (ed.), *Alexander the Great: the Main Problems* (Cambridge 1966).
Larsen, J. A. O., *Greek Federal States: Their Institutions and History* (Oxford 1968).
——, *Representative Government in Greek and Roman History* (Berkeley and Los Angeles 1955).
Tarn, W. W., *Alexander the Great* (Cambridge 1948).
Tarn, W. W., and Griffith, G. T., *Hellenistic Civilisation* (London 1952).
Wilcken, U., *Alexander the Great* (London 1932).

LIST OF ILLUSTRATIONS

49 Spartan warriors carrying their dead; Laconian cup from Tarquinii, sixth century B C. Staatliche Museen zu Berlin

50, 51 Euboea and cow; reverse and obverse of a coin of the Euboean League, c. 411–10 B C. Photos: Hirmer

52, 53 Apollo and lyre; reverse and obverse of a coin of the Chalcidian League, c. 412–10 B C. Photo: Hirmer

54 Combat between a Greek and an Asiatic; Attic *oenochoe* found in Italy, early fifth to fourth century B C. Musée du Louvre, Paris

55, 56 Turtle and tortoise; Aeginetan coins, late sixth century B C. Photos: Leonard von Matt

57 The Parthenon from the east. Photo: Edwin Smith

58 Two warships under sail; cup signed by Nikosthenes, from Cerveteri, c. 520 B C. Musée du Louvre, Paris. Photo: Hirmer

59 Lion's scalp; obverse of a coin of Samos, 454–453 B C. Photo: Hirmer

60 Warriors setting out; neck amphora by the Phiale painter, 440–430 B C. British Museum, London

61 Hector and Achilles fighting; detail of a *krater*. British Museum, London

62 Slave carrying pottery; terracotta statuette from Taranto. Antikensammlungen, Munich

63 Bread-seller; terracotta. Antikensammlungen, Munich

64 Women spinning and winding wool; scene on an Attic *pyxis*, 460–450 B C. British Museum, London

65 Model of a woman baking; Boeotian terracotta, early fifth century B C. British Museum, London

66 Comic actor dressed as a street vendor; statuette. Antikensammlungen, Munich

67 Cobbler making shoes to measure; vase from Rhodes, c. 500 B C. Ashmolean Museum, Oxford

68 A fishmonger's shop; vase from Lipari, fourth-third century B C. Collection Mandralisca, Cefalù. Photo: Leonard von Matt

69 Pottery painter; *krater*, fifth century B C. Ashmolean Museum, Oxford

70 Punishment of a slave; Lucanian *kalyx krater* by the Amykos painter, late fifth century B C. Staatliche Museen zu Berlin

71 Reveller and slave with lantern; terracotta. British Museum, London

72 Ploughing scene; Attic vase, early sixth century B C. British Museum, London

73 An armourer at work; interior of a *kylix*, fifth century B C. Ashmolean Museum, Oxford

74 Bronze greaves decorated with gorgons; from Ruvo, Etruria, 550–500 B C. British Museum, London

75 Trophy of arms showing a hoplite's armour; *hydria*. Musée du Louvre, Paris

76 A review of cavalry; red-figure cup by the Dokimasia painter, from Orvieto, c. 480–470 B C. Staatliche Museen zu Berlin

77 Foreparts of bull and lion; gold stater of Lydia, 561–546 B C. Photo: Hirmer

78 Lion with head reverted; Milesian coin, electrum, c. 575 B C. Photo: Hirmer

79 Beating down olives; scene on an amphora, sixth century BC. British Museum, London. Photo: Edwin Smith

80 Grape-picking; detail of a black-figure vase, fifth century BC. Musée du Louvre, Paris

81 Olive-press from Delos. Photo: French School at Athens

82 Ship bearing amphorae being brought to anchor; detail of a pottery jug, Cypriote, 700–600 BC. British Museum, London

83 Scene at a fountain; Attic vase, 510 BC. British Museum, London

84 Remains of the Enneakrounos at Athens, from the south-east. Photo: Agora Excavations

85 Terracotta drain-pipes from the Enneakrounos in the agora, Athens. Photo: Agora Excavations

86 Boundary stone of the Enneakrounos, Athens; last quarter of the fifth century BC. Photo: Deutsches Archäologisches Institut, Athens

87 Dionysus with the egg and cockerel; Boeotian terracotta found at Tanagra, c. 370 BC. British Museum, London. Photo: C. M. Dixon

88 Naked woman carrying outsize phallos; detail of a vase by the Pan painter. Staatliche Museen zu Berlin

89 Three ephebes in front of two herms: from an *oenochoe* or *olpe*. Musée du Louvre, Paris

90 Aspasia. Vatican, Sala delle Muse. Photo: Fototeca Unione

91 Herm of Socrates. National Museum, Naples

92 Stele of Cybele; second-first century BC. Musée d'Archéologie Borély, Marseilles

93 Mummy portrait; from Fayum, Egypt, second century AD. Antikensammlungen, Munich

INDEX